Teulu David Roberts, Lerpwl gan D.Ben Rees a Lawrence Holden

O LANRWST I LERPWL: BYWYDAU A CHYFRANIADAU DAVID ROBERTS (1806 – 1886) A'I FAB, JOHN ROBERTS (1835 – 1894)

gan D.Ben Rees

Cyhoeddiadau Modern Cymreig
Argraffiad Cyntaf : Mawrth 2018

Cyhoeddwyd gan y Wasg yn Lerpwl ar ran
Cymdeithas Etifeddiaeth Cymry Glannau
Mersi

Cyflwyniad a diolchiadau

Yr oeddwn yn ymwybodol iawn ers blynyddoedd o bwysigrwydd David Roberts, Hope Street, Lerpwl i hanes Cymry Lerpwl fel marsiandwr a chefnogydd y Methodistiaid Calfinaidd. Diwygiad Beddgelert a'i gweddnewidiodd a rhoddi iddo awydd gwasanaethu ei oes a'i Dduw. Ond deuthum i ar ei draws pan yn ymchwilio am radd MA i Fywyd a Gwaith Dr Owen Thomas, Pregethwr y Bobl fel y'i gelwid. Yr oedd David Roberts yn edmygydd mawr ohono, yn ei wahodd ef ag eraill i 'w gartref yn Lerpwl ac yn ddiweddarach yn ei Blas yn Abergele am wyliau i atgyfnerthu nerth y cennad ysbrydoledig. Pan yn gofalu ar ol Seiat yn Ysgoldy Fawr capel Princes Road byddai Owen Thomas yn gyson yn trosglwyddo yr awenau i David Roberts, y gwr a fu mor garedig tuag at y gost o adeiladu yr eglwys hardd. Etifeddodd ei fab John Roberts, y gwleidydd, yr un ymroddiad a theyrngarwch. A braint oedd ail greu y darlun ac atgyfnethu y gosodiad a wnaethum yn 1984 fod David Roberts yn un o'r lleygwyr pennaf a welodd yr enwad yn ei holl hanes. Gwaith da Cymdeithas Etifeddiaeth Glannau Mersi oedd ystyried cael dau ddiwrnod yn nechrau Mehefin i gofio David Roberts a'i deulu. Yr oeddwn cyn hynny wedi cyfarfod gyda Dr Lawrence Holden o Benbedw trwy garedigrwydd Ted Clement – Evans . Mewn cyfarfyddiad yn Aigburth amlinellodd Dr Holden a'i briod y byddai'n debygol y medrid dod a'r disgynyddion ynghyd i glywed y stori gan y byddai bron bob un ohonynt yn brin ei gwybodaeth o'r cyfraniad mawr a wnaeth y cwmni i fyd adeiladu yn ninas Lerpwl yn oes Fictoria. Trodd y cyfan yn llwyddiant a chafwyd Cyngerdd i gloi Dydd Sadwrn yng nghapel Elm Hall Drive ac Oedfa Grefyddol ddwyiethog ar fore Sul. Traddodais fy narlith yn Gymraeg a threfnwyd cyfieithydd ar y pryd , ac ar ol seibiant, cawsom yr hyfrydwch o wrando ar Dr Holden, un a gyfrannodd yn helaeth i fyd y Gyfraith yn y ddinas a hefyd i Brifysgol Lerpwl.

Diolchaf felly am y cyfle i olygu y gyfrol hon, i gyfraniad Dr L Holden, yn cefnogi fy ymdrech i rhoddi hanes y teulu ar gof a chadw, ac i Gymdeithas Etifeddiaeth Glannau Mersi am noddi'r digwyddiad a'r gyfrol trwy y Wasg, sef Cyhoeddiadau Modern Cymreig. Bu Dr Arthur Thomas yn help mawr gyda'r teipio a'r trefnu, ac felly hefyd David Fletcher gan osod y lluniau yn y testun. Diolchir i'r teulu am rai lluniau ac i Dr John G. Williams, Allerton, Lerpwl am ddewis o luniau sydd yn croniclo ein cyfarfodydd a'r teulu a ddaeth ynghyd i ganolfan y Cymry a chapel Bethel, Heathfield Road, Lerpwl.Mawr obeithiaf y caiff pawb a fydd yn darllen y testun yn Gymraeg a Saesneg fudd, gwybodaeth a phleser. Yn ddiolchgar, D.Ben Rees, (Golygydd), I Gorffennaf 2017.

O LANRWST I LERPWL: BYWYDAU A CHYFRANIADAU DAVID ROBERTS (1806 – 1886) A'I FAB, JOHN ROBERTS (1835 – 1894)

Ymhyfrydai David Roberts bob amser ei fod ef yn 'un o hogiau' Llanrwst yn Nyffryn Conwy. Tyddynwr oedd ei dad ar gyrion y dref a'i enw yntau oedd David Roberts. Priododd â merch John Owen, Dyffryn Aur, sef Mary ac o'r briodas hon ganwyd dau fab a merch. Ganwyd yr hynaf, David, gwrthrych ein hastudiaeth, ar Fawrth 6ed, 1806. Yr ail fab oedd Robert, a fu byw bywyd y filltir sgwâr. Hen lanc ydoedd a bu'n ffermio ar hyd ei oes yn Ffynnon Newydd. Margaret oedd enw'r ferch ac ar ôl priodi daeth i'w hadnabod fel Mrs. Margaret Blades.

Ni chyffyrddodd y Diwygiad Methodistaidd â'i rieni ac ni chafodd y bychan ei hyfforddi yn y ffydd. Bu farw ei dad yn 1814 pan oedd y mab hynaf ond yn wyth oed, gan roddi cyfrifoldeb mawr ar ei ysgwyddau i gynorthwyo ei fam ar y tyddyn. Cafodd fynediad i Ysgol Rad Llanrwst, nid oes tystiolaeth ar gael a dderbyniodd ef addysg yn y blynyddoedd cynnar. Yr oedd ysgol yn Nhrefriw dan ofal Evan Evans. Yno y bu y gŵr ifanc, Evan Evans, a adnabyddir yn well â'i enw barddol, Ieuan Glan Geirionydd, cyn mynd i Ysgol Rad Llanrwst. Mae'n bosibl i David Roberts ddilyn yr un llwybrau. Ond, yn 1818 y digwyddodd y foment fawr yn ei hanes a hynny yn ystod yr hyn a elwir Diwygiad Beddgelert. Cyfeiria ei ŵyr, John Herbert Roberts, Arglwydd Clwyd, yn ei hunangofiant, *Memoirs by John Herbert Roberts – Lord Clwyd* (Abergele, 1937) am brofiad Damascus a gafodd. Os am ddeall ei fywyd fel marsiandïwr ac arweinydd crefyddol yn Lerpwl mae'n rheidrwydd pwysleisio y profiad anghyffredin fel y sonia Williams Pantycelyn:

> Dyma'r bore fyth a gofiaf
> Clywais innau lais o'r nef
> Daliwyd fi gan wys oddi uchod
> Gan ei sŵn dychrynllyd ef.

Rhaid cofio fod Cymru, o 1735 i 1905, yn 'Wlad y Diwygiadau' a gwir y dywedodd Dr. R. Tudur Jones,

"I Gymry'r bedwaredd ganrif ar bymtheg yr oedd diwygiad yn un o elfennau sylfaenol ein Cristionogaeth".

Yn ystod plentyndod David Roberts o 1806 i 1819 bu diwygiadau mewn aml ardal, Bwlch-y-Groes, Gogledd Sir Benfro, Aberystwyth, Y Bala, Blaenannerch, Caernarfon, Treforys, Abertawe, Llanuwchllyn, Ysbyty Ifan, Llanwrtyd a Diwygiad Beddgelert. Cychwynnodd Diwygiad Beddgelert yn Ffermdy Hafod y Llan, Nant Gwynant, yn Awst 1817 ac erbyn y Nadolig yr oedd pob cartref yn ardal Nant Gwynant, Nantmor a Beddgelert wedi profi o'i rymusterau. Teithiodd David Roberts i Ddolwyddelan a chafodd ei ddwysbigo. Dywedodd Parchedig Francis Jones, Abergele, ffrind mawr iddo, y geiriau hyn, "Soniai yn aml, a chyda blas, am weddïau, pregethau a dylanwadau grymus yr adeg honno."

Teimlwyd effaith Diwygiad Beddgelert trwy Wynedd a rhai o siroedd y de, mor bell â Llanymddyfri ac un o'r rhai a ddaeth yn bregethwr grymus y diwygiad oedd Michael Roberts, Pwllheli. Ef, yn Sasiwn Llanidloes, fis Ebrill 1819, o flaen y Red Lion a gafodd oedfa anarferol ar Ddydd y Farn nes i gannoedd o bobl lewygu gan ofn a gweiddi "Beth a wnaf i fod yn gadwedig?" Yr oedd David Roberts wedi clywed Michael Roberts yn Llanrwst ac am glywed mwy o'i enau. Deuddeg oed oedd David Roberts pan gafodd ei argyhoeddi yn Nolwyddelan. Blwyddyn yn ddiweddarach gadawodd Ysgol Rad Llanrwst am Bwllheli ble cafodd waith mewn swyddfa cyfreithiwr yn y dref a ble'r arhosodd hyd 1822, cyfnod o dair blynedd. Bu'r tair blynedd hyn yn hynod o bwysig. Cafodd hyfforddiant manwl mewn materion cyfreithiol a mwynhâi y cyfle i bysgota, nofio a seiadu a chlywed dywediadau anghyffredin Michael Roberts (1780 – 1849), ysgolfeistr a phregethwr ym Mhwllheli. Yr oedd Roberts o feddwl praff a'i bregethu yn medru bod "yn rymus, trydanol a hyrddiol" i ddyfynnu Richard Thomas, Caernarfon. Gadawodd swyddfa'r cyfreithiwr yn 1822 gan fentro ar ei liwt ei hun i Lerpwl. Os hynny, daeth yn un ar bymtheg oed a dyna'r dystiolaeth a ddeuthum o hyd iddo yn yr ysgrifau a welais amdano ond, yn ôl ei ŵyr, ni ddaeth hyd 1824 pan oedd yn ddeunaw oed ac wedi derbyn cymynrodd o ewyllys perthynas i'w deulu. Ac, felly, nid ydym yn sicr.

Yn bersonol, rwyf yn tueddu am 1822 gan nad yw'r Arglwydd Clwyd yn medru rhoddi cyfrif am y ddwy flynedd goll megis yn ei hanes. Yn ôl nifer dda o Gymry tebyg iddo a ymfudodd i Lerpwl ym mlynyddoedd cynnar y bedwaredd ganrif ar bymtheg, dyna oed digon cyffredin. Oni ddaeth Elizabeth Davies neu Betsi Cadwaladr (1789 – 1866), gweinyddes yn y Crimea, i Lerpwl yn bedair ar ddeg oed i wasanaethu a glynu yn dynn wrth yr achos Methodistaidd yn Pall Mall? Pan ddaeth David Roberts i Lerpwl yn 1822 neu 1824 nid oedd yn adnabod neb.

Ond, sefydlodd yng nghyffiniau Capel Bedford Street a daeth i adnabod nifer o wŷr ifainc o'r un anian ag ef ei hun. Y cyntaf oedd Evan Rowlands,

Mann Street (1805 – 1828), athro eneiniedig, brodor o Lerpwl, a gŵr ifanc y meddyliai John Elias o Fôn y byd ohono. Cyhoeddwyd cofiant iddo yn 1829 gan ffrind arall o'r capel, John Roberts (1808 – 1880), a adnabyddir ym myd crefydd fel Minimus. Ganwyd ef yn Lerpwl yn ail fab i Richard Roberts, masnachwr nwyddau llong. Ar ôl gadael yr ysgol aeth i'r un fasnach â'i dad ond, ei brif ddiddordeb oedd Eglwys Methodistaidd Calfinaidd Cymraeg Bedford Street, lle yr etholwyd ef yn 1828 yn flaenor, gŵr ifanc 19 oed, yr ieuengaf y gwyddys amdano yn hanes yr enwad. I'r cwmni hwn o fechgyn ieuainc y daeth David Roberts. Un arall o'r cwmni oedd Josiah Hughes (1804 – 1840), Mansfield Street, a aeth allan yn 1830 yn genhadwr i Malacca. Ond, John Roberts a'i deulu oedd ffrindiau pennaf David Roberts a thrwyddynt hwy y cafodd ei gyflwyno i fyd marsiandïwyr coed.

1.   Y Marsiandïwr Coed

Cyflwynodd Richard Roberts ef i gwmni marsiandïwyr coed o'r enw David Hodgson, lle dechreuodd ei brentisiaeth. Rhaid cofio fod y Cymry yn llwyddo yn rhyfeddol yn y ddinas a oedd yn tyfu a datblygu. Yr oedd y cysylltiad rhwng Gogledd a Chanolbarth Cymru â Lerpwl yn amlwg erbyn 1830 â llawer iawn o'r defnyddiau ar gyfer adeiladu fel cerrig, brics, cynnyrch clai a llechi yn cael eu hanfon o'r cymunedau Cymraeg a Chymreig i lannau'r Merswy. Ond, yr oedd un deunydd angenrheidiol na fedrai Gogledd Cymru ei anfon, sef coed a phren. Yr oedd yn rhaid mewnforio y rhain o Ogledd America, yn arbennig Canada – Nova Scotia, Quebec, New Brunswick – Gogledd Ewrop, Danzig ac Ynysoedd y Caribî lle ceid mahogani, coed cedrwydd, ffawydden goch, pinwydden a choeden tîc (*teak*). Deuai'r coed a'r pren i dri porthladd – Lerpwl, Hull a Llundain. Yr oedd yr adeiladwyr Cymreig yn dra hoff o'r planciau o New Brunswick. Yn 1838, deuai 7.5 miliwn troedfedd ciwbig i Lerpwl ond cynyddodd erbyn 1852 i 34 miliwn ac awgryma hyn yr adeiladu aruthrol oedd i'w ganfod yn Lerpwl. Rhaid cofio fod y marsiandïwyr coed yn gwerthu i adeiladwyr mewn trefi eraill fel Manceinion, Bolton, mor bell â Bradford, Leeds a threfi y diwydiant cotwm fel Blackburn a Burnley.

Astudiodd David Roberts y diwydiant a'r fasnach yn drylwyr yn ystod ei brentisiaeth â chwmni D. Hodgson. Meistrolodd manylion y busnes a daeth yn gryn arbenigwr, gan arbenigo ar fahogani. Yn wir, o fewn pum mlynedd o weithio yn y diwydiant, ni fyddai Hodgson yn dychmygu prynu coed mahogani heb ofyn barn y prentis. Ac yntau yn cwblhau ei brentisiaeth digwyddodd dau beth arall a alwodd David

Roberts yn "weithredoedd rhagluniaeth". Yn gyntaf, oherwydd anawsterau yn y Baltig, aeth y cwmni yn fethdalwr ac, yn ail, derbyniodd lythyr oddi wrth gwmni cyfreithwyr yn Llanrwst yn ei hysbysu iddo dderbyn cymunrodd arall, swm o £300 y tro hwn. Gwelwyd y gallu oedd ganddo ar waith yn ddiymdroi, gan fod ceffylau a pheiriannau i drin y coed yn mynd ar werth a, heb golli amser, sefydlodd ei gwmni ei hun, prynodd y ceffylau, peiriannau a'r wagenni a chymerodd iard goed yn Hill Street. O'r foment honno ymlaen ni edrychodd yn ôl o gwbl. Llwyddodd ei fusnes a bodlonodd ei gwsmeriaid a gwnaeth ddewis da yn ei fywyd priodasol.

Soniais am Minimus ei ffrind ac, wrth fynd i'w gartref, daeth i adnabod ei chwiorydd Jane, Miriam ac Anne. Tair merch hardd a golygus. Syrthiodd ef mewn cariad â Jane; priododd Anne â David Charles yr Ail (1803 – 1880) o Gaerfyrddin, gweinidog adnabyddus yn ei ddydd. Priodwyd David Roberts â Jane Roberts yn 1832 a bu'n ffodus o'i briod. Priodas dda. Meddai ar feddwl cryf, medrai ostegu unrhyw storm â'i ddylanwad yn fawr ar yr aelwyd. Wrth ddychwelyd o'u mis mêl yn y cerbyd, eisteddai hi yn nesaf at y gyrrwr. Y diwrnod hwnnw, sef Hydref 15fed, 1832 yr oedd y Dywysoges Fictoria yn dychwelyd o Blas Newydd, Llanfairpwll ar ôl bod yng nghwmni'r Marcwis/Ardalydd. Fel y deuai cerbyd y Robertsiaid at Westy y Wenynen (Bee Hotel) yn Abergele, gwelodd y dyrfa hwy gan gredu mai Jane Roberts oedd Fictoria. Cawsant eu croesawu yn dywysogaidd a churo dwylo diddiwedd!

Nid oedd David Roberts yn fodlon ar un iard goed. Agorodd un arall yn 1834 yn Fonteroy Street, yn ogystal â Hill Street. Aeth i bartneriaeth â John Jones a chymerodd iard goed arall yn Dale Street.

Yn yr ugeinfed ganrif gwerthwyd yr iard goed hon ac adeiladwyd Siambrau Westminster ar y fangre. Adnabyddid y cwmni fel Jones a Roberts. Yn 1835, ganwyd etifedd i David a Jane Roberts a galwyd ef yn John a daeth yntau, maes o law, i ddilyn llwybrau ei dad.

Yn 1848 newidiwyd yr enw i David Roberts a'i Gwmni a daeth William Jones yn bartner iddo am rai blynyddoedd. Agorwyd iard goed arall yn Fox Street, gan brynu peiriannau newydd o Sbaen i dorri coed yn blanciau ar gyfer yr adeiladu. Erbyn hyn, oddeutu 1850, yr oedd 70 o farsiandïwyr coed wedi'u sefydlu yn Lerpwl, â llawer iawn ohonynt yn nwylo'r Cymry. Gellir enwi cwmnïau fel Joseph Owen a'i Feibion a'i iard goed yn St. Anne Street; Walker and Roberts ond, y pwysicaf o bell ffordd, oedd David Roberts a'i Fab. Daeth cwmnïau eraill a sefydlwyd gan Gymry yn y chwedegau fel John Hughes a'i Gwmni ac Isaac Evans a'i Gwmni.

Daeth Fox Street yn bencadlys y ffyrm ac ehangwyd eto pan brynwyd melin lifio (saw mill) yn Derby Road, Bootle. Ymddeolodd John Jones o'r cwmni yn 1856 a blwyddyn yn ddiweddarach ymunodd ei fab, John Roberts, â'r cwmni ac ar ôl pum mlynedd o brentisiaeth cafodd ei wneud yn bartner gan i William Jones farw yn 1860. Yr oedd angen partner ar David Roberts ac yr oedd ef a'i fab ar delerau da, yn fwy fel dau frawd na thad a mab. Gofalodd John Roberts gynllunio y felin lifio yn 1861 a'i galw'n Cambrian Saw Mills yn Derby Road pan bwrcaswyd y cyfan gan Gwmni Rheilffordd Lancashire and Yorkshire, penderfynodd y cwmni adeiladu melinau eraill y tro hwn yn Esk Street a Primrose Road, Bootle. Yn 1864 ymunodd y mab-yng-nghyfraith, D. Lloyd Davies, â'r cwmni a bu ef ar y bwrdd rheoli hyd 1872. Agorwyd cangen arall o'r busnes yn Church Street, Penbedw, a bu yno hyd 1883 pan symudwyd yr iard i Bridge Street.

Dan weledigaeth John Roberts, mentrwyd i fyd yr adeiladu yn gynnar yn y chwedegau a dyma ddechrau adeiladu teyrnas fawr arall yn ystod y saith deg mlynedd nesaf hyd tridegau'r ugeinfed ganrif. Adnabyddid David Roberts fel gŵr prydlon, cwbl onest (onest fel y dydd) ac arbenigwr ar fahogani, un o'r rhai pennaf ym myd coed ym Mhrydain. Nid oes gennym wybodaeth am y melinau hyn na'r iard goed oedd yn ei feddiant. Ond, pan aeth iard goed cwmni Cymreig R.L. Lloyd ar dân yn 1879, cawn syniad o faintioli yr adeiladau a berthynai hefyd i David Roberts. Safai iard goed R.L. Lloyd ar gongl Dexter Street a Park Lane. Yr oedd yn adeilad pedwar llawr, 130 troedfedd o hyd, ac o'i fewn siop y seiri, peiriannau llifio, yr holl blanciau a bu'n rhaid brwydro am awr a hanner â'r goelcerth. Yr oedd R.L. Lloyd a David Roberts yn adnabod ei gilydd yn dda.

Ymffrostiai David Roberts yn ei berthynas dda â'i weithwyr. Erbyn 1875 yr oedd 400 yn gweithio i'r cwmni yn Lerpwl a Phenbedw. Ar ôl adeiladu tai crand yn Abergele byddai'r tad a'r mab yn gwahodd yr holl weithwyr a'u gwragedd a'r plant i dreulio diwrnod yn yr haf yn eu plith. Ymffrostiai David Roberts fod pobl o bob enwad yn gweithio yn yr iardiau a'r melinau coed a phobl oedd yn pleidleisio i'r Blaid Dorïaidd a'r Blaid Ryddfrydol.

2. **Y Calfinydd Methodistaidd**

Fel y gwelwyd, bu Capel Bedford Street yn gartref ysbrydol o'r wythnos gyntaf y cyrhaeddodd Lerpwl o Lanrwst. Yr oedd Bedford Street wedi ei amgylchynu gan gapeli o'r enwadau eraill; symudodd yr Annibynwyr Cymraeg yno o Greenland Street. Yn 1838, daeth yr Eglwys Fethodistiaid (Wesleaid) i Hill Street yn 1833 ac yn 1829 ymsefydlodd y Bedyddwyr Cymraeg yn Heath Street cyn symud i Stanhope Street yn 1834. Gwelodd David Roberts Gapel Bedford Street yn cynyddu fel y gwelodd yr ierdydd adeiladu llongau ar lan yr afon. Gweithiai cannoedd lawer yn yr ierdydd hyn, cyfran dda yn Gymry Cymraeg. Bu'n rhaid ailadeiladu Capel Bedford Street a'i ailagor Gwener y Groglith (Ebrill 9fed, 1841). Bu dyfodiad y Parchedig John Hughes (1796 – 1860) i fyw yn 31 Mount Street yn 1838 yn gaffaeliad enfawr i achos y Methodistiaid Calfinaidd yn Lerpwl ac ymaelododd ef a'i deulu yn Eglwys Bedford Street a dod yn ffrindiau mawr â David Roberts a'i deulu, oedd yn gymdogion yn Hope a Mount Street. Gŵr amryddawn dros ben oedd John Hughes, awdur tair cyfrol bwysig ar *Hanes Methodistiaeth Cymru 1851 – 1855* ac fel y dywed R.T. Jenkins, llyfrau sydd heddiw eto'n anhepgor. Bu ei ddylanwad yn bwysig ar ei gyd-weinidog, Henry Rees, ar David Roberts a'i fab, John Roberts, a ddaeth yn fab-yng-nghyfraith iddo, ac yn gefn i Dr. Lewis Edwards, Y Bala, a'r Parch. Roger Edwards, Yr Wyddgrug.

Etholwyd David Roberts yn flaenor y tro cyntaf yn 1836 ond, oherwydd bod amheuaeth am gymeriad gŵr o'r enw William Williams, Frederick Street, perswadiodd ef y tri arall a etholwyd i sefyll lawr er mwyn cadw'r gynulleidfa heb ei rhannu. Dwy flynedd yn ddiweddarach, ym mis Mawrth 1838, fe'i dewiswyd yn flaenor am yr eildro. Y tro hwn, ef yn unig a etholwyd. Yr oedd hi'n anrhydedd iddo a gwelodd yr Eglwys yn tyfu o 480 o aelodau yn 1841 i 515 yn 1856, 574 yn 1860 a 765 yn 1865. Y cyfanswm cyfan, aelodau ar brawf a phlant oedd 952 â David Roberts yn dra dylanwadol ac mewn perffaith gydgord â'i weinidog, Parchedig David Saunders. A phan benderfynwyd adeiladu Eglwys Gadeiriol y Methodistiaid Calfinaidd Cymraeg, David Roberts oedd y prif ysgogydd. Dewiswyd ef yn Llywydd y Cyfeisteddfod Adeiladu ac o fewn dyddiau yr oedd wedi penderfynu cael y capel ar y ffordd hardd, a elwid yr adeg honno, Princes Road â'i *boulevard* llydan. Dyma'r rhan harddaf o'r ddinas a phwy oedd yn berchen y tir, wel David Roberts a'i Feibion. Prynodd ddarn helaeth yn enw David Roberts a'i Fab gan Iarll Sefton. Hwy oedd perchen y tir o amgylch, yr hyn a elwid yn Gaeau'r Senedd (Parliament Fields). David Roberts a'i Feibion oedd berchen y rhanbarth eang i fyny am Croxteth Road, Millet Road i Smithdown Road. Gwerthodd y tir i Gymry adeiladu, gan osod amod na ellid adeiladu tafarn ar un rhan o'r stad ac, felly, tafarn Brooke House oedd yr unig un o Upper Parliament Street i Penny Lane.

Gosodwyd y dasg i benseiri, Meistri W. a C. Audsley, gynllunio'r adeilad. Cafwyd cyfarfod mawr yng Nghapel Bedford Street, Ionawr 24ain, 1865 a daeth y cannoedd ynghyd. Syfrdanwyd pawb pan ddywedodd David Roberts fod y capel yn mynd i gostio deng mil o bunnoedd. Ond, mewn gwirionedd, pan orffennwyd, roedd y draul cymaint dwywaith. Yng Nghofiant Henry Rees, o waith Dr. Owen Thomas, rhoddir adroddiad o'r cyfarfod, un o'r "rhai mwyaf brwdfrydig a llwyddiannus a gynhaliwyd erioed."

Yr oedd David Roberts yn benderfynol fod rhaid i'r Cymry ddangos i'r ddinas ei bod hwy â chyfraniad pwysig i'w gyflawni o ran pensaernïaeth, crefydd, addysg grefyddol a phregethu'r efengyl. Yr oedd ef ei hun yn ymgorfforiad o'r Calfinydd ar ei orau, o fewn deugain mlynedd yr oedd y llanc deunaw oed wedi dod yn filiwnydd trwy ragluniaeth Duw ac ethig Brotestanaidd o waith.

Dywedodd David Roberts y cyfan yn ei frawddeg ysgubol,

"Nid oes gennym y fath air ag 'amhosibl' yn yr iaith Gymraeg mewn cysylltiad ag achosion crefydd."

Gŵr arall a daniwyd y noson honno oedd Henry Rees, gweinidog Capel Chatham Street. Yr oedd ei unig ferch, Anne, wedi priodi â Richard Davies, Treborth, Bangor, teulu Methodistaidd cyfoethog arall. Rhannwyd tocynnau drwy'r gynulleidfa i nodi yr addewid o arian at y cynllun uchelgeisiol. Cymerodd hyn dri chwarter awr ac aeth Henry Rees mor hy â gofyn i'r Cadeirydd, David Roberts, faint oedd ef am ei roi. Atebodd David Roberts braidd yn ddistaw ei fod yn "gobeithio crafu ynghyd bedwar ffigwr". Meddyliodd Henry Rees mai pedwar cant o bunnoedd oedd ganddo ar gyfer y gronfa. Ond, nid dyna a roddodd David Roberts – rhoddodd y swm anhygoel o £1,272-17-0, cyfystyr â dwy filiwn yn 2016. Yr ail orau oedd John Roberts, ei fab, sef y swm o £637-2-0. Y nesaf, £351 gan Thomas Davies, Berry Street. Llwyddodd David Roberts gael Iarll Sefton roddi £200 a'i gymydog, John Lewis, Hope Street, y swm o £150-10-0 a'i fab-yng-nghyfraith, D. Lloyd Davies wedi rhoddi swm sylweddol hefyd.

Dywed yr hanesydd J. Hughes Morris,

"Diau na chyfranesid symiau mor hael yn flaenorol i hyn tuag at unrhyw achos ynglŷn â'r cyfundeb, a dywedir bod rhodd Mr. David Roberts o fil o bunnoedd – rhodd na chlybuasid am ei chyfelyb ymysg y Cymry o'r blaen – wedi bod yn foddion i godi safon cyfrannu yn yr eglwys."

Gosodwyd carreg sylfaen Capel Princes Road bnawn y Llungwyn, Mehefin 5ed, 1865, ychydig ddyddiau ar ôl i'r llong *Mimosa* hwylio â 164 o deithwyr a deunaw morwr ar y daith wyth mil o filltiroedd i'r Ariannin a Gwladfa Patagonia. Ond, daeth mwy o bobl i osod y garreg sylfaen nag yr aeth at lan yr afon i weld y *Mimosa* yn ymadael ond, tra mae Princes Road yn ysgerbwd trist heddiw, mae Cymry Patagonia yn ffynnu ac yn agor ysgolion Cymraeg o'r Gaiman i'r Andes. Daeth oddeutu tair mil i Princes Road a gwelwyd mawrion y pulpud yn ei morio hi, Dr Lewis Edwards, David Saunders, Dr. Owen Thomas, Henry Rees, W.C. Roberts, Efrog Newydd. Pwy gafodd y fraint o osod y garreg sylfaen? Un yn unig. Y pen blaenor a chyflwynwyd iddo drywel arian yn dwyn arni gerfiad o'r Capel newydd a'r geiriau,

"Cyflwynwyd gan Ferched Ieuainc Cynulleidfa Bedford Street i David Roberts, Ysw., ar yr achlysur o osodiad carreg sylfaen Capel Princes Road ganddo, Mehefin 5ed, 1865."

Costiodd yr holl waith ar yr adeiladau y swm o £19,633-8-5 a bu'n rhaid byw â dyled o dros naw mil am rai blynyddoedd ar ôl ei agor yn 1868. Hwn, yn ôl y papurau a'r cylchgronau, oedd yr adeilad harddaf, tu mewn ac allan, yn Lerpwl a'r cyffiniau. Dyma'r gampwaith, ni lwyddodd y Cymry fel hyn, yn Llundain nac Efrog Newydd, y Wladfa nac Awstralia. Nid oedd pawb yn bles â'r ysblander. Arweiniwyd gwrthryfel gan Richard Jones, Gibson Street, siaradwr huawdl a gŵr o'r dosbarth gweithiol a'i bryder ef oedd y ffenestri lliw, a oedd yn sawru o babyddiaeth. Tawelwyd ef mewn byr o dro gan David Roberts a ddadleuai fod Duw a chenedl y Cymry yn haeddu'r gorau. Pan ddaeth Owen Thomas i weinidogaethu yn y capel newydd yn 1871 cafodd 61 Hope Street ymwelydd cyson. Y nos Wener o flaen Sulgwyn 1873, cynhaliwyd cyfarfod arall i ddileu'r ddyled a derbyniwyd y noson honno addewidion am £4,400. Cyfrannodd David Roberts eto (ef yn unig) swm arall o fil o bunnoedd a'i fab, John, y swm o bum cant. Llawenydd mawr i David Roberts oedd fod Eglwys Bedford Street wedi ethol ei fab, John, yn flaenor yn 1867 a chawsant flynyddoedd lawer o gydweithio yn y swyddogaeth.

David Roberts

Rhydd yr Arglwydd Clwyd atgofion gwerthfawr am ei daid, David
Roberts, fel gŵr crefyddol a oedd yn byw mewn amser o newidiadau
helaeth ym mywyd y Cymry yn yr hen wlad ac ar lannau'r Merswy.
Chwaraeodd ran bwysig ym mywyd crefyddol Cymry Lerpwl, yn
arbennig yn sefydlu Cymdeithas Genhadol y Methodistiaid Calfinaidd a
hynny ar ôl i Minimus, ei frawd-yng-nghyfraith, drefnu cyfarfod
cyhoeddus yn Festri Capel Rose Place nos Wener, Ionawr 31ain, 1840
dan lywyddiaeth y seraff bregethwr Henry Rees. Bu'n haelionus a
gweithgar i'r Gymdeithas Dramor a dilynwyd ef yn hyn o beth gan ei fab,
John. Pan yn dathlu hanner can mlynedd o fynd allan i India, cynhaliwyd
cyfarfod arbennig yng Nghapel Methodistiaid Calfinaidd Abergele dan ei
lywyddiaeth. Soniodd John Roberts am yr angen o sefydlu Coleg
Diwinyddol yn Khasia, cenhadaeth i Sylhet a gwaith meddygol.
Casglwyd £165 yn yr oedfa, can punt gan John Roberts, hanner canpunt
gan ei fab, J. Herbert Roberts, a phymtheg punt gan weddill y
gynulleidfa. Diolch am y Robertsiaid y noson honno yn Abergele!
Bu David Roberts ar flaen y gad ag addysg. Meddiannodd yr un awydd â
Syr Hugh Owen (1804 – 1881), Llundain, a chyfoeswr. Cydweithiodd yn
fawr â Hugh Owen. Yn 1865 yr oedd ef a Hugh Owen a'r Parchedig
John Phillips (1810 – 1867) yn hyrwyddwyr y mudiad a sicrhaodd
sefydlu'r Coleg Normal ym Mangor. Trwy'r tri hyn yn bennaf y
sicrhawyd coleg i hyfforddi athrawon cymwys ar gyfer Ysgolion
Brutanaidd a Thramor. Coleg yr Hen Gorff yn ei hanfod oedd y Coleg
Normal a chostiodd yr adeilad £13,000. Ni chafwyd ond £2,000 gan y
Llywodraeth a bu John Phillips a David Roberts yn gyfrwng i gasglu
£11,000 i gyfarfod â'r cyfanswm. David Roberts oedd cefnogwr blaenaf

Coleg y Bala, coleg i baratoi bechgyn ieuainc ar gyfer y Weinidogaeth Gristnogol ac enwad y Methodistiaid Calfinaidd. Ysgogydd y cynllun hwn oedd John Elias o Fôn. Deuai John Elias yn gyson i Bedford Street, yn wir yr oedd ei ail wraig, Y Fonesig Bulkeley, gweddw Syr John Bulkeley, Presddafed, Môn, yn aelod yn y capel. Daeth David Roberts i'w hadnabod ac yr oedd yn bresennol ym mhriodas John Elias a'r Fonesig Bulkeley yn Eglwys Anglicanaidd Dewi Sant, Russell Street, Lerpwl, ar Chwefror 10fed, 1830. Nid rhyfedd fod Lewis Edwards, Prifathro'r Coleg, yn barod i ddod i gyfarfodydd Bedford Street, gan y gwyddai mai ei gefnogwr blaenaf o ran arian oedd David Roberts. Meddyliai David Roberts y byd o bob cangen o Eglwys Princes Road. Ar Awst 6ed, 1869 ymwelodd Ysgol Sul Princes Road, ar ei wahoddiad ef, ag Abergele. Daeth bron i bum cant o'r disgyblion a'r athrawon ar y trên a chawsant eu harwain gan seindorf arian o'r orsaf i'r capel newydd, Mynydd Seion. Yno, yr anerchwyd hwy gan Peter Williams, Lerpwl, masnachwr llwyddiannus. Dilledydd ydoedd a gwnaeth ffortiwn. Yr oedd ef a David Roberts yn bennaf ffrindiau. Ei feddrod ef ym Mynwent Smithdown yw'r talaf o bell ffordd. Yr oedd y garreg fedd hardd i ddweud stori llwyddiant bydol y brawd a ddaeth o Brymbo i Lerpwl. Y siaradwr arall oedd y Parchedig R. Roberts, Brynhyfryd. Yna, cafwyd gorymdaith i ail gartref David Roberts a'i briod, sef Tanrallt. Yno, ar y lawnt gwelwyd pabell eang, ysblennydd a chinio braf wedi ei baratoi ar gyfer y pum cant. Yr oedd David Roberts a theulu Bryngwenallt, sef ail gartref ei fab, yno i'w croesawu. Ni arbedwyd unrhyw gost. Ar ôl cinio aed am dro trwy erddi Tanrallt ac yna trwy Blas Bryngwenallt ac allan i'r wlad am Lanfairtalhaearn. Daeth y dorf yn ôl i'r babell am de lle paratowyd cacennau a danteithion o bob math. Erbyn hyn, yr oedd y brenin yn eu plith, y Parchedig Owen Thomas, Lerpwl, ac yn diolch am yr haelioni. Yn ystod ei gyfnod yn Princes Road, deuai ef yn gyson i aros ar aelwyd Tanrallt a Bryngwenallt. Byddai wrth ei fodd. Dywed y papur lleol am y digwyddiad, "Yr oedd yr olwg arnynt (hynny yw pobl Princes Road) yn anrhydeddus a boneddigaidd. Gwelsom lawer ymweliad cyffelyb o dro i dro ac ni welsom erioed dyrfa mor luosog yn dangos mor barchus yr olwg arni." Dychwelodd y dyrfa luosog, barchus i orsaf Abergele. Gadawsant Tanrallt am 5.30 er mwyn dal trên 6.15 o'r gloch.

Bnawn trannoeth, gwahoddwyd Ysgol Sul Methodistiaid Calfinaidd i Danyrallt i fwynhau te yn y babell. Sonia Arglwydd Clwyd amdano fel crefyddwr a'r hyn a arhosodd yn ei feddwl o'i blentyndod, David Roberts fel gweddïwr ymysg aelodau'r teulu. Byddai'n arwain addoliad teuluaidd

yn Hope Street ac Abergele. Yna, yn ail, ei gyfraniad yn y seiat ar nos
Sul, yn codi'r gynulleidfa i dir uchel gyda'i sylwadau buddiol. Byddai'n
rhoi allan i ganu yn ddieithriad yr emyn,

Braint, braint
Yw cael cymdeithas gyda'r saint,
Na welodd neb erioed ei maint:
   Ni ddaw un haint byth iddynt hwy;
Y mae'r gymdeithas yma'n gref,
   Ond yn y nef hi fydd yn fwy.

Ac yna ei ddawn i arwain yn ddoeth a sensitif yn yr wythnos, yn
arbennig y Seiat Brofiad na chofia neb ohonom ni erbyn hyn
bwysigwydd na sylwedd y cyfarfod ysbrydol hwnnw. Galwai Dr. Owen
Thomas yn gyson ar David Roberts i'w gynorthwyo.

   Mr. David Roberts, ewch chi i'r llawr am ychydig funudau; rwy'n
gweld bod hwn a hwn yn eistedd yn y fan acw; mae wedi bod yn wael;
ewch i gael gair ganddo. Ac yna,

   Mae hwn a hwn yn eistedd tu ôl iddo; fe gollodd ei fab yn ddiweddar;
deudwch air wrtho. Cymerai yntau ei hun at y dasg am yr hanner awr
olaf. Mynych y treulid awr a hanner i ddwy awr mewn Seiat.

   Yr oedd David Roberts wedi ei drwytho yn emynau William Williams
(1717 – 1791), Pantycelyn, un o gewri y Diwygiad Methodistaidd. Nid
yn unig yn ei emynau ond ym marwnadau y Pêr Ganiedydd. Cymerodd
ran amlwg yn cefnogi adeiladu capeli Saesneg yn yr enwad ac ef a'i fab a
dalodd am adeiladu Capel Pensarn, ger Abergele yn 1879 a'i gyflwyno i'r
Cyfundeb. Er ei fod ef yn Gymro o argyhoeddiad, sylweddolai fod angen
gofalu ar ôl y di-Gymraeg yng Nghymru. Ysgwyddodd gyfrifoldeb o
fewn y Gymdeithas Genhadol Gartrefol, yr Achosion Saesneg, Trysorfa y
Gweinidogion, Cymdeithas y Beibl ac, ar farwolaeth David Davies,
Mount Gardens, yn 1860, penodwyd ef yn Ymddiriedolwr y Genhadaeth
Dramor a Thrysorydd er cynorthwyo cenhadon methedig yn Assam,
ynghyd â gweddwon a phlant amddifad. Mil o bunnoedd oedd yn y
Gronfa yn 1843 ond, pan fu farw, yr oedd dros £49,000.

   Gwnaed Tysteb iddo a chyflwynwyd y cyfan ar Fawrth 9fed, 1886 yn
Hope Street a daeth un ar bymtheg o wŷr amlwg Gogledd Cymru a
Lerpwl ynghyd dan arweiniad Dr. Owen Thomas a Dr. John Hughes
(1827 – 1893), Gweinidog yn Lerpwl ers 1857 a mynych ymwelydd â
Hope Street. Trosglwyddwyd llun hardd ohono ef a darluniau hefyd o

Gapeli Princes Road, Mynydd Seion, Pensarn, Y Coleg Normal, Bangor, a golygfeydd o Danyrallt. Ffrâm pedair troedfedd a chwe modfedd o hyd wrth dair troedfedd o led a hwnnw wedi ei addurno mewn aur ac arian. Llofnodwyd gan flaenoriaid amlwg a chyfoethog fel Edward Davies, unig fab y cyfalafwr o Fethodist, David Davies (1818 – 1890), Llandinam. Yr oedd David Roberts mewn iechyd da a mwynhaodd y diwrnod hwnnw yn fawr iawn.

Ond, o fewn chwe mis bu farw David Roberts, a hynny ar nos Sul, Hydref 3ydd, 1886. Ei ddymuniad oedd cael marw ar y Sul gan iddo ef dyna Ddydd yr Arglwydd a'r tro olaf y bu yn y capel oedd Sul olaf mis Awst. Cofier ei fod erbyn hynny yn flaenor yn Lerpwl ers hanner can mlynedd ac Abergele ddeng mlynedd ar hugain. Trefnwyd yr angladd dros ddau ddiwrnod. Y diwrnod cyntaf oedd dydd Iau, Hydref 7fed yn Abergele – cerdded o Danyrallt i Fynydd Seion dan ganu,

> Mae nghyfeillion adre'n myned
> O fy mlaen o un i un

a, hefyd,

> Bydd myrdd o ryfeddodau ar doriad bore wawr.

Cafwyd pump teyrnged iddo ac yr oedd pymtheg cant wedi ymgynnull, yn eu plith Emrys ap Iwan. Caewyd pob siop a masnachdy yn Abergele a thynnwyd y llenni ar ffenestri'r tai. Cariwyd yr arch ar ysgwyddau gweithwyr y ddau blasdy, Tanyrallt a Bryngwenallt, i'r capel ac o'r capel i'r orsaf i ddal trên pedwar o'r gloch i Lerpwl ar gyfer trannoeth. Dydd Gwener daeth miloedd o drigolion Lerpwl, oddeutu pum mil, a dygwyd y teulu o Hope Street i Princes Road gan chwech o gerbydau. Gorlanwyd y Capel, na fyddai wedi ei adeiladu oni bai amdano ef, ac yr oedd miloedd tu allan. Anerchwyd y gynulleidfa gan Dr. Owen Thomas, Thomas Levi (1825 – 1916), Gweinidog Eglwys y Tabernacl, Aberystwyth, Golygydd *Trysorfa'r Plant;* Francis Jones, ei weinidog yn Abergele, a Dr. John Hughes. Yn bresennol Prifathro y Coleg Normal, Parchedig Daniel Rowlands (1827 – 1917); Yr Athro Hugh Williams (1843 – 1911), Athro Groeg a Mathemateg Coleg y Bala; Yr Athro Ellis Edwards (1844 – 1915), mab Roger Edwards, Yr Wyddgrug, ac Athro Lladin, Groeg a Saesneg yng Ngholeg y Bala, Yr Athro Henry Jones (1852 – 1922), Athro

Athroniaeth Coleg y Brifysgol Gogledd Cymru, Bangor; Parchedig William James (1833 – 1905), Gweinidog Capel Moss Side, Manceinion, gŵr blaenllaw iawn yn ei gyfundeb, a'i feddyg, Dr. Gee, Sgwâr Aberconwy.,Lerpwl. Gwelwyd dim ond un Aelod Seneddol yn bresennol, J. Bryn Roberts. Yr oedd y prif alarwyr yn niferus – ei fab, meibion-yng-nghyfraith, ei frawd, Robert Roberts, a'i wyrion, saith ohonynt, a cheid cerbydau yn cynrychioli y fasnach goed, blaenoriaid Sasiynau y De a'r Gogledd a mawrion Cyngor Dinas Lerpwl. Gwnaed yr arch o dderw caboledig.

Cerddwyd o Princes Road i fynwent Sant Iago gan y Gweinidogion, blaenoriaid Princes Road, cynrychiolwyr yr Ysgolion Sul a sefydliadau cyhoeddus. Yr oedd y llanc o Lanrwst wedi dod yn un o brif fasnachwyr Lerpwl a gwnaeth y gorau o ddau fyd. Ond, fel y dywedwyd yn *Y Goleuad*, Hydref 16eg, 1886 yr oedd yn "ddyn da, yn ddyn Duw ac yn ddyn y bobl". Meddai ar ddeallusrwydd bywiog, treiddgar, natur gynnes a chyflym, ar rai adegau yn gynhyrfus ond, sylfaen fawr ei gymeriad oedd ei grefydd Galfinaidd Fethodistaidd. Neges Dr. Owen Thomas i'r holl alarwyr oedd "byddwch yn debyg i David Roberts". Gadawodd yn ei ewyllys (a wnaed ar Fawrth 4ydd, 1886) £60,698-1-7, swm enfawr yn 2018. Yr ysgutorion oedd John Roberts a'r ŵyr John Henry Roberts. Gadawodd i'w ferch, Elisabeth Anne Henry, priod y Parchedig Henry Jones Henry, set arian orau o lestri te a choffi; Mary Robinson, nith ei ddiweddar briod, £100 a swm o £3,000. Ei fab yn etifeddu'r gweddill ar ôl i'r merched, Elizabeth Ann Henry a Jane Lloyd Davies a'u teuluoedd gael rhyngddynt £22,000 a £28,000 i'w fuddsoddi.

Ganwyd John Roberts yn 1835 yn Lerpwl a chafodd gartref Fethodistaidd trwyadl, ei ail gartref oedd Capel Bedford Street lle y daeth, fel ei dad a'i daid, Richard Roberts, a'i ewythr Minimus a'i dad-yng-nghyfraith, John Hughes, Mount, yn arweinydd. Yn addysgol, derbyniwyd ef i Ysgol Liverpool Institution a'i anfon i ysgol fonedd yn Brighton fel â ddigwyddodd i Winston Churchill. Meddai ar allu anhygoel, yn arbennig mewn mathemateg a dylai fod wedi cael cyfle mynd i Rydychen neu Gaergrawnt. Ond, yr oedd ei dad angen cymorth yn y busnes a oedd yn tyfu yn aruthrol. Yn ystod ei gyfnod yn Brighton, cafodd fantais fawr o fynychu Capel Trinity, lle pregethai yr anfarwol bregethwr, Frederick William Robertson (1816 – 1853) a elwid yn 'Robertson of Brighton'. Daeth i enwogrwydd mawr er iddo farw yn 37 mlwydd oed. Yng Nghapel Bedford Street y cyfarfu â'r ferch a ddaeth yn wraig iddo, Catherine Tudor Hughes, merch y Parchedig a Mrs. John Hughes, Mount Street.

Catherine Roberts (nee Hughes)

Cartrefwyd yn 63 Hope Street yn agos at rieni y ddau ohonynt. Yn wahanol i'w dad, ymddiddorodd y mab mewn gwleidyddiaeth y Blaid Ryddfrydol. Nid oedd y Rhyddfrydwyr mor weithgar yn Lerpwl ag y dylent. Pobl gyfoethog oedd arweinwyr y blaid â'r mwyafrif ohonynt yn Anglicaniaid neu Undodiaid. Hwy, yr Undodiaid, oedd arweinwyr pennaf y Rhyddfrydwyr. Meddylier am William Rathbone y Pumed (1787 – 1867), diwygiwr a darfu ar Gyngor y Dref yn 1820 pan gadwodd ei het ar ei ben, yn unol ag ethos y Crynwyr, wrth gynnal munud o dawelwch ar farwolaeth y Brenin Siôr IV. Trawyd yr het oddi ar ei ben ond, atgoffodd bawb yn y siambr fod rhyddid i fynegi eich hunan yn hawl na ddylid ei daflu i ffwrdd. Erbyn 1837 yr oedd yn Faer y Dref ond, mae'n amlwg nad oedd Rhyddfrydiaeth fel y gwelai yn Lerpwl yn apelio ato. Yr oedd ei Gymreictod yn ei ddenu i feddwl am gyflwr Cymru a'i buddiannau. Cynnyrch y capel oedd John Roberts ac nid cynnyrch clybiau a chymdeithasau dyngarol. "The Chapels," meddai'r hanesydd Ieuan Gwynedd Jones, "in creating their own values, produced men who embodied those values and so crated their own *élite*." Nid oedd neb a gynrychiolai'r elît hwnnw yn well na John Hughes, Mount; Roger Edwards a Lewis Edwards. Dyma ddechrau'r bendefigaeth newydd, yr hyn a elwir, yn bendefigaeth Ymneilltuol. Wedi'r cyfan yr oedd Cymru yn llawer mwy crefyddol na dinas Lerpwl. Cofier mai cynnyrch Diwygiad Beddgelert oedd David Roberts a gwelodd ef a'i fab Ddiwygiad 1859 ar waith. Cryfhawyd y capeli yn ddirfawr, gan gynnwys Capel Bedford Street a chafodd John Roberts ei gyffroi i weithredu. Ef oedd un o brif sylfaenwyr Cymdeithas Ddiwygiadol Gymraeg (Welsh Reform Association) a siaradodd â dylanwad mawr yn y cyfarfod bythgofiadwy yn Amphitheatre Lerpwl ym mis Mai 1868. John Bright oedd y prif areithiwr ond, John Roberts oedd yr enw ar wefusau'r dorf a lanwodd yr Amphitheatre. Gwelodd Bright a phawb arall a oedd yno y potensial yn y gŵr ifanc 33 mlwydd oed. Apwyntiwyd ef yn fuan i fainc yr ynadon yn Lerpwl ac yna un Sir Ddinbych, gan fod ei dad wedi cael ail gartref yn Abergele yng nghanol y pumdegau. Y flwyddyn honno, gwelwn fod John Roberts wedi cynnig enw George Osborne Morgan (1826 – 1897) fel un o'r ddau aelod dros Sir Ddinbych; y llall oedd Syr Watkin Williams-Wynn. Yr oedd George Osborne Morgan yn esiampl da i John Roberts, ei flaenoriaethau oedd mesurau yn ymwneud ag Ymneilltuaeth grefyddol a Chymraeg. Yn 1870, o ganlyniad i'r hyn a ddigwyddodd yn angladd y Parchedig Henry Rees, Lerpwl, ym Mhorthaethwy y flwyddyn cynt, cyflwynodd fesur i alluogi unrhyw enwad Cristnogol gynnal gwasanaeth ym mynwentydd y plwyf. Daeth â hwn ymlaen yn y Tŷ Cyffredin am ddeg tymor seneddol yn olynol a llwyddo yn y diwedd i'w gael yn Ddeddf yn 1880. O 1870 i 1878 soniwyd droeon am John Roberts fel Ymgeisydd Seneddol ond, yn haf 1878 daeth y cyfle ar Orffennaf 3ydd ond, ni fu'n hawdd. Yr oedd gŵr arall, E.K. Muspratt, â'i lygaid ar sedd Bwrdeistrefi y Fflint; siaradwr campus â'i gartref yn Trelawney House, Y Fflint. Disgynnodd y goelbren ar John Roberts i ymladd yr Is-etholiad. Cynhwysai'r sedd saith tref, sef Y Fflint, Owrtyn, Treffynnon, Caerwys, Yr Wyddgrug, Caergwrle a Llanelwy. Daeth y sedd yn wag trwy farwolaeth Ellis Eyton, Aelod Seneddol ers 1874. Ei wrthwynebydd oedd gŵr o deulu adnabyddus, Philip Pennant Pennant. Yr oedd gan y Torïaid eu cadarnleoedd, yn arbennig dinas leiaf Prydain, Llanelwy, a hefyd, Owrtyn. Enillodd John Roberts â mwyafrif o 125 pleidlais. Fel capelwr o fri, gwyddai John Roberts am yr awydd angerddol ym mhlith yr Ymneilltuwyr o bob enwad i sancteiddio'r Sul fel diwrnod o addoli ac addysgu. Dim ond y capel a'r dafarn oedd ar agor ar y Sul yng Nghymru ac nid oedd croeso hyd yn oed i'r trên redeg o Ferthyr i Gaerdydd ar y Sul. Fel y dywedodd un hen law,

"The great ones of the country had got rich by the labour of the working classes and they grudged them the little relaxation which a Sunday trip gave them."

Yr oedd 77% o drethdalwyr Gogledd Cymru o blaid cau'r tafarnau. Yn wir, arwyddodd 793 o dafarnau'r gogledd dros gau. Dim ond 153 a arwyddodd yn erbyn. Ym mis Medi 1879, rhoddodd John Roberts yn y Senedd ei fod yn cyflwyno mesur i gau tafarnau ar y Sul yng Nghymru. Darllenwyd y mesur am y tro cyntaf ar Chwefror 6ed, 1880 a chefnogwyd ef gan Henry Richards, Apostol Heddwch; Samuel Holland (Meirionnydd); Henry Vivian, Aelod Seneddol Morgannwg, a'r ddau o Ddinbych, Watkin Williams ac Osborne Morgan. Yn ei araith ar Fehefin 30ain, yn yr ail ddarlleniad, soniodd y byddai'r Ddeddf yn dilyn Mesur Cau Tafarnau Iwerddon 1878. Yr oedd holl Aelodau

Seneddol Cymru o blaid, nid oedd gan y tafarnwyr ffrindiau yn eu plith a bu'n rhaid dibynnu ar aelod Seneddol Bridport, Edward Warton, wrthwynebu'r mesur. Yr oedd ef yn anobeithiol, gan mai ei ddadl oedd fod Cymru yn rhan o Loegr. Pasiodd yr ail ddarlleniad heb rannu'r Tŷ a rhoddwyd i'w ddadansoddi yn y pwyllgorau erbyn Gorffennaf 1880. Bu'n rhaid aros hyd 1881 i'r Ddeddf gael y gefnogaeth angenrheidiol, dim ond Arglwydd Emlyn, a gynrychiolai Sir Gaerfyrddin, a anghytunai. Crisialwyd y ddadl yn berffaith gan Osborne Morgan,

"I think it is time that people should understand that in dealing with Wales you are really dealing with an entirely distinct nationality, a nationality more distinct than that of the Scotch or Irish, because Wales is separated from England not merely by race and by geographical boundaries but, by a barrier which interposes at every turn of life – I mean the barrier of language."

Ond, bu'r ymgyrch yn llwyddiannus oherwydd cefnogaeth William Gladstone, y Prif Weinidog, a siaradodd am chwarter awr o blaid y Mesur. Pasiwyd y mesur â mwyafrif o 147 a dim ond dwy bleidlais ar bymtheg yn erbyn.

Bu'n rhaid i John Roberts ymladd etholiad arall yn 1880 a bu'n fuddugoliaeth arall iddo dros yr un gwrthwynebydd, Philip Pennant Pennant. Gwelwyd John Roberts a'i briod mewn cerbyd agored yn gofyn am gefnogaeth. Y canlyniad:

John Roberts (Rh) 2039
P.P. Pennant (C) <u>1468</u>
Mwyafrif   571

Yn ôl y *Cambrian News* trôdd holl drigolion Abergele allan i'w groesawu pan gyrhaeddodd ar y trên o'r Fflint. Canwyd llu o ganeuon yn y ddwy iaith yn ystod yr ymgyrch:

Pennant, like Brutus, may honourable be,
But he's not the man to be Flintshire's MP
So work, boys for Roberts, the friends of working men
And never rest contented till you have him up again.

Ac yn y Gymraeg:

Mae'r nefoedd Ryddfrydol yn bloeddio'n gytûn,
Rhowch Pennant i gadw, John Roberts yw'r dyn.

Daeth profedigaeth fawr i'w ran ar Fedi 13eg, 1880 pan fu farw ei briod, Katherine Tudor Roberts, yn 43 mlwydd oed. Gwelsom hi wrth ei ochr yn yr is-etholiad a'r etholiad. Mynychodd bob cyfarfod, bu'n canfasio ym mhob un o'r saith canolfan a sgwrsio â'r etholwyr mewn modd gyfeillgar, garedig.
Treuliodd haf 1880, diwedd mis Gorffennaf a dechrau mis Awst, ym Mryngwenallt a mwynhaodd gwmni ei phlant. Ar Fedi'r ail, aeth i'w hystafell wely a'r diwrnod canlynol ganwyd eu deuddegfed plentyn, Cecil. Yr oeddynt wedi colli dau blentyn, Mary Ellen a Gladys, o'r dwymyn goch (scarlet fever). Perswadiodd hi John Herbert a Trevor, ei frawd, fynd am wyliau i Ardal y Llynnoedd â ffrindiau o Gapel Princes Road – Harrison Jones a J.G. Evans – ac ewythr i'r bechgyn. Llogwyd bwthyn yn Clappergate ac ar Fedi 18fed aeth pob un ohonynt i Helvellyn a chael diwrnod wrth eu bodd. Pan ddychwelont i'r bwthyn, yr oedd y perchennog, Miss Allenby, yno gyda'r hyn a elwid yr adeg honno yn bapur coch, sef telegram. Agorwyd a chael y newydd fod eu mam wedi marw. Dychwelwyd i Abergele ar y trên a daeth David Roberts i'w cyfarfod. Ni all John Herbert Roberts adrodd mwy o'r hanes ac ni allaf weld bai arno, gan ei fod wedi colli Mam a fu mor ofalus ohonynt. Gofynnwyd i Dr. Owen Thomas ofalu am yr arwyl a chymerodd ei frawd, Dr. John Thomas, Gweinidog Annibynwyr Cymraeg Lerpwl, ran. Ymysg y galarwyr tu allan i'r teulu gwelwyd Richard Davies, AS Môn, a theulu Treborth.

Yr oedd gan John Roberts dri chartref – 67 Lancaster Gate, Hyde Park yn Llundain; Hope Street ac, yn ddiweddarach, West Dingle yn Lerpwl, a Bryngwenallt yn Abergele. Nid oedd hi'n hawdd cadw sedd Bwrdeistrefi'r Fflint er ei holl lafur a'i fedrusrwydd. Gofalai ar ôl busnes Lerpwl â'i frodyr ar ôl dyddiau ei dad a swcrodd y mab, John Herbert, i ystyried gyrfa wleidyddol. Nid oedd pall ar ei garedigrwydd i'w weithwyr a phobl dlawd Lerpwl ac Abergele. Gweithiodd yn ddyfal dros Gronfa yr Achosion Saesneg o fewn yr enwad yng Ngogledd Cymru a bu'n Drysorydd y Gronfa. Gofalai bob Calan gynnig calennig i bobl dlawd Abergele. Derbynient baced o de a chwe cheiniog ac oren i bob plentyn a alwai arnynt. Dosbarthwyd yn nechrau 1894 fil o baced chwarter pwys o de.

Safodd Pennant yn ei erbyn am y trydydd tro yn etholiad 1885 ac yr oedd hi'n anodd arno heb ei briod yn ystod yr ymgyrch. Enillodd â mwyafrif bach – 123 yn unig:

John Roberts (Rh) 1835
P.P. Pennant (C) <u>1713</u>
Mwyafrif 123

Blwyddyn yn ddiweddarach bu'n rhaid sefyll eto mewn etholiad ond, y tro hwn, ni safodd P.P. Pennant. Oherwydd cwestiwn o hunan lywodraeth i Iwerddon, rhwygwyd y Blaid Ryddfrydol yn ddwy a safodd Syr H.M. Jackson fel Rhyddfrydwr Unoliaethol (Liberal Unionist). Cafodd John Roberts fwy o fwyafrif y tro hwn:

John Roberts (Rh) 1827
Syr H.M. Jackson (LU) <u>1403</u>
Mwyafrif   424

Yr oedd enw da iddo fel gwleidydd a fedrai siarad yn raenus ar bob achlysur a rhoddi cyfrif o'i stiwardiaeth. Ef oedd yr unig Aelod Seneddol yn hanes y Fwrdeistref a fyddai'n ymweld â phob tref i adrodd ei stori fel Seneddwr. Derbyniodd gefnogaeth gref gan Weinidogion Ymneilltuol fel y Parchedigion David Oliver, Treffynnon; D.M. Jenkins, Josiah Thomas, Lerpwl; E. Lloyd Jones, Y Rhyl; Robert Jones, Yr Wyddgrug, a'r pregethwr a'r nofelydd Daniel Owen, awdur *Rhys Lewis* ac *Enoc Hughes*. Yn 1889 treuliodd ddau fis yn teithio yn yr Unol Daleithiau ac aeth â'i fab, John Herbert, ag ef. Pan ddychwelodd, aeth ef a'i gyfaill o Lerpwl, Samuel Smith, Rhyddfrydwr haelionus arall, ar hyd ei etholaeth i sôn am ei argraffiadau o'r wlad fawr ar draws yr Iwerydd. Cymerodd hi dair wythnos i groesi Môr yr Iwerydd i Efrog Newydd.

John Roberts, Aelod Seneddol

Penderfynodd John Roberts roddi'r gorau i'w etholaeth oherwydd cyflwr ei iechyd yn 1891 ar ôl tair blynedd ar ddeg o wasanaeth i'r Blaid Ryddfrydol a'r Mudiad Dirwest. Llawenydd mawr iddo oedd trosglwyddo'r awenau i John Herbert Lewis (1858 – 1933), cyfreithiwr yn Lerpwl a Chadeirydd cyntaf Cyngor Sir y Fflint (1889). Un o Sir y Fflint ydoedd, o Fostyn, yn or-nai i'r diwinydd Thomas Jones, Dinbych. Bu'n Aelod Seneddol dros Fwrdeistrefi'r Fflint 1892 – 1906.

Daeth y diwedd yn ddisymwth ac annisgwyl yn hanes John Roberts a bu farw nos Sadwrn, Chwefror 24ain, 1894 yn West Dingle, Lerpwl, ar ôl iechyd symol am beth amser. Bu'r angladd, nid yn Lerpwl fel yn hanes ei dad, ond yn Abergele ac fe'i gosodwyd ym medd ei briod. Gwnaeth ei ewyllys ar Dachwedd 29ain, 1892 a gwerthusid ei ystâd bersonol yn £163,395-6-9. Yr ysgutorion oedd ei feibion John Herbert, Aelod Seneddol, a David Trevor, West Dingle. Derbyniodd John Herbert y swm o ddeugain mil, ynghyd â lluniau, platiau, dodrefn, deunydd y tŷ, y ceffylau a'r cerbydau. Yr oedd D. Trevor i dderbyn deng mil o bunnoedd. Bwriadai roddi cyfranddaliadau cyfartal i weddill ei blant ond, bod rhai John Herbert ddwywaith yr hyn a dderbyniai y chwe mab arall a'r dair ferch. Nodir fod mil o bunnoedd i'w drosglwyddo i'w fab, Arthur Lloyd, Cwmni Siwgr, Louisiana, Yr Unol Daleithiau.

Nid oedd **dynasty** y Robertsiaid ar ben o bell ffordd, yn wir, yr oedd David Trevor yng ngofal David Roberts a'i Gwmni ar ôl i J. Herbert ennill sedd fel Aelod Seneddol a chafwyd oes aur arall y cwmni yn yr ugeinfed ganrif. Cadwyd arwyddair y cwmni yn fyw – arwyddair answyddogol adeiladwyr Lerpwl – "Cyfiawnder oddi wrth Owen Elias (brenin yr adeiladwyr) a thrugaredd oddiwrth David Roberts a'i Gwmni, cymwynaswyr eiddgar ym myd moes, dirwest a Christnogaeth."

LLYFRYDDIAETH FER

CYMRAEG

i)   D. Densil Morgan, *Lewis Edwards*, Cyfres Dawn Dweud, Caerdydd, 2009

ii)   John Gwynfor Jones a Marian Beech Hughes (Golygyddion), *Hanes Methodistiaeth Calfinaidd Cymru, Cyfrol III, Y Twf a'r Cadarnhau (c. 1814 – 1914)*, Caernarfon, 2011

iii)   J. Hughes Morris, *Hanes Methodistiaeth Liverpool,* Cyfrol 1, Lerpwl, 1929

iv)   D. Ben Rees, *Pregethwr y Bobl: Bywyd a Gwaith Owen Thomas*, Lerpwl a Phontypridd, 1979

SAESNEG

i)   Martin Doughty, *Building the Industrial City*, Leicester, 1986

ii)   J.R. Jones, *The Welsh Builder on Merseyside*, Liverpool, 1946

iii)   John Herbert Roberts, *Memoirs by Lord Clwyd,* Abergele, 1937 (Privately Printed)

iv)   D. Ben Rees, *Local and Parliamentary Politics in Liverpool from 1800 to 1911, Studies in British History*, Volume 55, Lewiston, Queenston, Lampeter, 1999

GŴYL DAVID ROBERTS – COFIO CEWRI OES VICTORIA

Cynhaliwyd yr ŵyl i ddathlu bywyd a gwaith David Roberts a'i ddisgynyddion ar y pen wythnos Mehefin 11-12,2016 gyda darlithiau yn y bore yng Nghapel Bethel a'r Ganolfan Gymraeg, cyngerdd yn yr hwyr yng nghapel Elm Hall Drive a gwasanaeth o ddiolchgarwch bore Sul ym Methel. Trefnwyd yr ŵyl gan Gymdeithas Etifeddiaeth Cymry Glannau Mersi dan arweiniad Dr D. Ben Rees, ac mewn cydweithrediad gyda Dr Lawrence Holden, Penbedw yn cynrychioli disgynyddion David Roberts.

Paratowyd arddangosfa ddiddorol ganddo gan gynnwys siart o achau y teulu ers dyddiau David Roberts, lluniau o ddau gartref y teulu gerllaw Abergele sef Tanrallt a Bryngwenallt , a nifer o eitemau diddorol eraill yn enwedig y ddogfen gyfreithiol drawiadol yn dyrchafu John Herbert Roberts yn Farwn Clwyd yn 1919.

Rhan o'r gynulleidfa y darlithoedd / Part of the audience at the lectures

Rhoddwyd y ddarlith gyntaf yn yr Iaith Gymraeg ar David Roberts (18061886) a'i fab John Roberts, A.S. (1835-1894) gan Dr D Ben Rees. Cefais y fraint o gyflwyno'r darlithydd oedd wedi gweithio'n galed ar yr ymchwil gan mae ychydig iawn oedd yn wybyddus am y marsiandwr coed a'i fab y gwleidydd Rhydfrydol . Trefnwyd gwasanaeth cyfieithu ar y pryd gan y Gymdeithas ac fe werthfawrogwyd y cyfleuster yma yn fawr gan nifer dda o'r teulu oedd wedi dod i'r Ŵyl o bob rhan o'r wlad.

Yn dilyn ei fagwraeth yn Llanrwst daeth David Roberts i Lerpwl yn ddyn ifanc iawn yn 1822 ac ymhen ychydig flynyddoedd roedd wedi sefydlu cwmni yn mewnforio coed gan arbennigo mewn coed mahogani.Aeth y fusnes o nerth i nerth. O 'r cychwyn bu yn aelod o gapel Bedford Street ac yn fuan etholwyd ef i'r Sedd Fawr a bu yn flaenor weddill ei oes, hyd ei farwolaeth yn 1886. Ei ddymuniad mawr oedd adeiladu capel, teilwng o safle y Cymry yn y ddinas. Sicrhaodd ei benderfyniad, gan mai hwy oedd berchen y tir a brynodd oddiwrth Iarll Sefton a'i gefnogaeth ariannol, adeiladu capel urddasol Princes Road. Agorwyd y capel yn 1868.

Ymunodd ei fab John Roberts yn y busnes a'i ddatblygu ymhellach gan gydweithio gyda'r pensaer dylanwadol Richard Owen . Yn 1878 etholwyd ef yn Aelod Seneddol Rhyddfrydol dros Bwrdeisdrefi Sir Fflint ac fe wnaeth gyfraniad sylweddol i sicrhau y mesur cau y tafarnau ar y Sul yng Nghymru erbyn 1881.

Y Goeden Deulu / Family tree

Yn dilyn egwyl cafwyd darlith ddiddorol arall gan Dr Lawrence Holden ar ddau o ddisgynyddion David Roberts sef, David Trevor Roberts a John Herbert

Roberts, A.S., yn ddiweddarach y Barwn Clwyd. a hefyd dau wleidydd arall sef teulu Caine a Syr Herbert Lewis .Canolbwyntiodd David Trevor Roberts ar ddatblygu y cwmni ac yn 1906 etholwyd John Herbert Roberts yn Aelod Seneddol dros Sir Fflint, a'i ddyrchafu yn Farwn Clwyd yn 1919.

Bwriedir cyhoeddi y ddwy ddarlith hynod bwysig yma mewn llyfr yn y dyfodol agos, a byddwn yn hysbysebu yn ol ein harfer yn yr Angor..

Yn yr hwyr bu cyngerdd cofiadwy yng nghapel Elm Hall Drive gyda Côr y Porthmyn o ardal y Rhewl, ger Rhuthun. Dan arweiniad Erfyl Owen, cyflwynwyd y rhaglen apelgar gan Gwynfor Jones. Cafwyd unawdau gan John Jones, Geraint Evans, John Thomas, Wyn Jones, Brian Hughes a Eirlys Jones. Yn ystod yr egwyl rhoddwyd datganiad gan Mrs Rhiannon Liddell ar y piano o ddarn a gyfansoddwyd gan Mervyn Roberts, trydydd mab Arglwydd Clwyd. Yn dilyn gair o werthfawrogiad gan Mrs Alice Brown, Glasgow ar ran y teulu, cafwyd datganiad gwefreiddiol gan Barnaby Brown ar y '*triplepipes*'.

Barnaby Brown   Alice Brown

Roedd yn offeryn digon cyffredin yn y byd Celtaidd yn y canol oesoedd, ac mae'r defnydd ohonno yn parhau yn Sardinia. Llywyddwyd gan y Dr D.Ben

Rees yn ei afiaith ei hun ac yn hyfryd o ddi-rybudd mynegodd Mr Brian Thomas, Mossley Hill , aelod o Bwyllgor Gwaith y Gymdeithas, werthfawrogiad didwyll o weledigaeth ein Llywydd Dr Ben ar hyd y blynyddoedd ac yn arbennig gyda Gwyl David Roberts ac eiliwyd hyn gan gyfeirio at y criw bach sydd yn ysgwyddo y cyfrifoldeb gan Ted Clement – Evans, Aigburth. O blith chwiorydd y Pwyllgor Gwaith sef Dr Pat Williams, Mrs Nan Hughes Parry a Mrs Beryl Williams porthwyd y porthmyn yn unol a thraddodiad Cymry Lerpwl gyda lluniaeth blasus. Noson gofiadwy iawn.

Y Cyngerdd a'r cantorion o ddyffryn Clwyd / the concert and the choir from the vale of Clwyd

Ar fore Sul bu gwasanaeth o ddiolchgarwch ym Methel dan arweiniad y gweinidog, Dr Ben Rees, gyda Mrs Rhiannon Liddell wrth yr organ. Cymerwyd rhan gan aelodau o bwyllgor Cymdeithias Etifeddieth Cymry Glannau Mersi,mewn gwasanaeth a baratowyd yn ofalus ac a argraffwyd ar gyfer y gynulleidfa deilwng a ddaeth ynghyd. Roedd hynny yn wir ym mhob cyfarfod a gafwyd .

Arthur Thomas

David Roberts of Liverpool and his family
By D.Ben Rees and Lawrence Holden

To Liverpool from Llanrwst
The lives and contribution of David Roberts (1806-1886) and his sons John Roberts (1835-1894), David Trevor Roberts (1861- 1935) and
John Herbert Roberts, Lord Clwyd (1863-1955)

by D. Ben Rees and Lawrence Holden Modern Welsh Publications, Allerton, Liverpool 2018 First edition: March 2018

Presented to the descendants of David Roberts in 2018

**Published on behalf of
Merseyside Welsh Heritage Society
by Modern Welsh Publications,
Allerton, Liverpool 18**

Contributors

Dr D.Ben Rees

Dr Lawrence Holden

Preface

It was a fascinating task to research the Roberts story. It had so many different angles. There were certainly "larger that life" characters and much telling detail but the underlying story of the pressures that drew so many Welsh people to Liverpool and how they created a genuinely good community of Welsh speakers in what must have been, for them, an alien city is a powerful one.

Extremes of wealth and squalor and a dynamic mercantile class whose morality was based upon the slave trade must have been challenging to the Welsh immigrants with their deep faith strengthened by series of "revival' and vigorous growth of dissenting chapels. Yet they built for themselves a civilised community that truly flourished and in due course made a great contribution to Liverpool especially in building the sort of houses that Liverpool needed and could afford.

In doing this they made, in various senses, Liverpool the capital of much of Wales. This applied in thought, in religious development, in education, in enterprise and especially in Liberal politics. It was the deep involvement of members of the Roberts family in that community that gave them the spirit to make their mark nationally and led the contribution of the four "family" MPs at the height of Welsh Liberalism.

It was a real pleasure to meet with and learn from members of the Merseyside Welsh Heritage Society and I am very grateful for the all the help they gave. It was also a very good to see so many members of my wife's family enjoying their encounter with the Welsh language and culture.

The Welsh community in Liverpool have much to be proud of and to celebrate .I hope the lectures given at the Roberts festival in June 2016 will help to keep these achievements alive.

Lawrence Holden June
2017

Chapter 1
The lives and contribution of David Roberts (1806-1886) and his son John Roberts (1835-1894)
By D.Ben Rees

1. David Roberts - an introduction.

David Roberts was very proud of being 'a Llanrwst lad' and it was on the outskirts of this historic market town in the Conwy valley that he was brought up, on his father's smallholding. His father, also named David Roberts, had married Mary, one of the daughters of Dyffryn Aur farm, and together they had two sons and a daughter. David, the subject of this article, was the eldest and was born on the 6th of March 1866. The second son, Robert, was very much a home bird and remained a bachelor, living out his secluded, nearly a recluse life, farming the nearby Ffynnon Newydd. The daughter's name was Margaret, who in married life was known as Mrs Margaret Blades.

The parents were not influenced by the eighteenth century Methodist Revival and David was not brought up in the Calvinistic Methodist way of life.. The father died in 1814 when David was no more than eight years of age, an event that brought upon him a huge responsibility to help his mother on the smallholding. He became a pupil at Llanrwst Grammar School, normally known by the name Ysgol Rad Llanrwst (the Llanrwst Free School). There is no record of his having had any schooling in his early years, but there was at the time a school in Trefriw, attended by one Evan Evans, a man more familiar to us as the poet Ieuan Glan Geirionnydd, who also went later to Llanrwst Grammar School. It is possible that David Roberts' education took the same route.

David Roberts' life changed for ever in 1818, during what is known as the Beddgelert Revival. David Roberts' grandson, John Herbert Roberts - Lord Clwyd – writes about this 'Damascus conversion' in his autobiography 'Memories' (Abergele 1937). In order to understand David Roberts' life as a businessman and Christian leader one needs to be aware of this event and of the enormous significance it had for him. In the words of the hymnwriter William Williams, Pantycelyn:

Dyma'r bore, byth mi gofiaf,
 Clywais innau lais y nef.
Daliwyd fi drwy wys oddi uchod

Gan ei sŵn dychrynllyd ef

[*This is that unforgettable morning Upon*
which I heard the voice of heaven.
I was captured, summoned from above
By its tremendous terrible sound.]

One needs to keep in mind that Wales in the period 1735 to 1905 was *the* nation
of revivals. To quote the great scholar and theologian Dr. R Tudur Jones: 'For
the people of Wales in the 19th century, revival was a basic, core element of
Christianity.' Between 1806 and 1819, during the years of David Roberts'
childhood, there were revivals in many parts of Wales: in Bwlch- y- Groes,
north Pembrokeshire, Aberystwyth, Bala, Blaenannerch, Caernarfon, Morriston,
Swansea, Llanuwchllyn, Ysbyty Ifan, Llanwrtyd and of course, Beddgelert.

The Beddgelert Revival began in August 1817 in the farmhouse of Hafod y
Llan, Nant Gwynant. By Christmas, every household in the parishes of Nant
Gwynant, Nanmor and Beddgelert had been seriously affected by the
outpouring of the Holy Spirit. It was on a visit to Dolwyddelan that David
Roberts came under its influence and into the presence of God. The Reverend
Francis Jones, Abergele, a close friend of David Roberts in his adult life, has
said that 'He would speak often and with relish about the prayers, the sermons
and the powerful presence of the Holy Spirit felt at this time.'

The effect of the Beddgelert revival was felt throughout Gwynedd and in
counties further south as far away as the town of Llandovery in
Carmarthenshire. The Revival brought the ministry of many a long-forgotten
preacher into the limelight. One of them was Michael Roberts (1780-1849
) of Pwllheli. In the mid Wales town of Llanidloes on the 11th of April 1819,
during the Presbyterian Association meeting , Roberts gave a sermon in front of
the Red Lion tavern on the subject of the Judgement Day. The response was
dramatic. Hundreds fainted from fear of Judgement Day or called out "What
can we do to be saved?" David Roberts had heard Michael Roberts preach in
Llanrwst and was keen to hear more of his unique style of preaching. He was
twelve years of age when he dedicated himself to God in Dolwyddelan. A year
later he left Llanrwst Grammar School for Pwllheli where he secured a post as a
clerk at a solicitor's office. He remained there until 1822, a period of three very
important years in his development when he received a thorough grounding in
matters of the law. In his own spare time he enjoyed swimming and fishing
and particularly the chapel Society meetings where he absorbed the powerful

teaching of Michael Roberts. Michael Roberts was a school master and preacher of great intelligence, and his preaching - in the words of a twentieth century preacher Reverend Richard Thomas of Caernarfon - was 'powerful, electrifying, moving' Various accounts relate how David Roberts left the solicitor's office in 1822 to venture on his own to Liverpool. If this is true, he would have been no more that sixteen years of age. However, according to his grandson he didn't come to Liverpool until 1824 when he would have been eighteen and in receipt of a legacy from the will of a friendly relative. There is some doubt, therefore, as to the actual date of his arrival in Liverpool, though I myself tend towards 1822 as the most likely given that Lord Clwyd is unable to account for the intervening two years. And, according to chapel histories a large number of Welsh people moved to Liverpool in the early years of the nineteenth century at a young age. They were in similar circumstances to those of David Roberts. So it is possible that he came at the age of sixteen. That was quite common. A good example would be that of Elizabeth Davies, better known as Betsi Cadwaladr (1789-1860) the famous Crimean War nurse and staunch member of the Methodist cause in Pall Mall Liverpool , who was taken into service in Liverpool at fourteen years of age, after running away from her Calvinistic Methodist father in Bala.

When David Roberts came to Liverpool in 1822 - or 1824 - he knew no-one, but found himself a home within the catchment area of Bedford Street Chapel. There he became acquainted with a number of young men of the same interests, nature and temperament as himself. The first of this group was Evan Rowlands (1805-1828) of Mann Street, a gifted teacher, a native of Liverpool and a young man of whom John Elias the famous Revival preacher from Anglesey thought a great deal of him. The second friend at the chapel was none other than John Roberts (1808-1880) better known in religious circles as Minimus. It was he who published a biography of Evan Rowlands after his early death in 1829. In the biography he states that Evan Rowlands was born in Liverpool like he was. After all Minimus himself was the second son of Richard Roberts a ships chandler, and after leaving school he went into the same business as his father. His main interest, however, was in writing hymns and attending Bedford Street Welsh Calvinistic Methodist Chapel where, in 1828, he was elected an elder - and at nineteen years of age he is the youngest ever to my knowledge to be elected to the position of Elder within the chapel community. It was into the company of young men of this calibre that David Roberts found himself within a few weeks of arriving in Liverpool. Another religiously minded young man was Josiah Hughes (1804-1840) of Mansfield Street, who in 1830 went as a missionary to Malacca. in the Far East. However,

David Roberts' closest friends were John Roberts and his family, and it was through them that he was introduced to the world of the timber merchant.

2. David Roberts the timber merchant

David Roberts was introduced by his mentor Richard Roberts to the Liverpool timber merchant company of David Hodgson. It was here that he began his apprenticeship in the business. It is important to remember that Welsh people were a phenomenally successful part of nineteenth century Liverpool life. In 1830 the city was growing and developing, and its links with North and Mid Wales were strong and much of the material that was used to construct the important port - the stone, slate and clay products - came from these areas' where the Welsh speaking communities were thriving.. There was however one essential raw material that Wales was not able to provide, and that was timber. Timber had to be imported from north America, largely from Canada, Nova Scotia, Quebec and New Brunswick, and also from northern Europe and the Caribbean - the last of these being the source of woods such as mahogany, cedar, red beech and pine and teak. The wood was imported through three ports, namely Liverpool, Hull and London, and Welsh building contractors were particularly fond of timber from New Brunswick. In 1838 7.5 million cubic feet of timber was imported through Liverpool; by 1852 this had increased to 34 million cubic feet, a figure indicative of the immense building projects in the hands of the Welsh in the growing town. (Liverpool became a city in 1880 when it became a diocese within the Anglican Church). Keep in mind as well that Liverpool timber merchants also sold timber to building contractors in other towns and cities especially to Manchester, Bolton, Bradford and Leeds for example, as well as to cotton towns such as Blackburn and Burnley.

During his apprenticeship at David Hodgson's, David Roberts made a thorough study of the timber industry and trade. He not only mastered the finer points of the business but he also became an expert on mahogany. Indeed it is said that David Hodgson, a mere five years after taking on David Roberts, wouldn't dream of buying mahogany without first consulting his young apprentice. As he was finishing his apprenticeship there occurred two events that David Roberts refers to as 'acts of providence'. First of all David Hodgson's timber company was bankrupted as a result of problems in the Baltic. Secondly, David Roberts received a letter from a solicitor in Llanrwst notifying him that he was the beneficiary of a further legacy, in this story a sum of £300. He was quick to realise the opportunity that this presented him. Hodgson's horses and machinery were all up for sale and he moved quickly to buy them and establish his own company at the timber yard on Hill Street. From this point on there was no looking back for David Roberts. He satisfied his customers, his business flourished, and he chose an excellent wife. One has already refered to David Roberts' friend Minimus. On David Roberts frequent visits to his friend house he got to know his sisters, Jane, Miriam and Anne, all three of them beautiful and attractive young women. Of these, Anne was to marry the Reverend David Charles (1803-1880), a famous Calvinistic Methodist minister from Carmarthen. But it was with Jane that David Roberts fell in love, and they got married in 1832. It was a marriage literally made in heaven and he was fortunate in his choice of helpmate. Jane Roberts was strong minded, able to weather any emotional storm, and had great influence over the household. On their return from their honeymoon Jane chose to sit next to the coachman, and that on the day, the 15th of October 1832, when Princess Victoria was on her way back to London from a visit to the Marquis of Anglesey's home at Plas Newydd near Llanfair P.G. As the Roberts' coach approached the Bee Hotel in Abergele, the crowd, waiting there to see the Princes mistook Jane Roberts for Victoria. The welcome the Roberts' carriage received was truly fit for a future queen and they were greeted by wave after wave of clapping and cheering from the Welsh royalists!

David Roberts was known for his promptness and his honesty in everything he did. He was also known as an expert in Mahogany, becoming one of the foremost among the experts in the whole of Britain. He was not content with owning only the one timber yard and in 1834 opened a second one in Fontenoy Street. He then entered into a partnership with John Jones, forming the company known as Jones & Roberts and took on a further timber yard in Dale Street. This timber yard was sold during the twentieth century and the Westminster Chambers were built on the site. In 1835 Jane gave birth to a son, John, who was later to inherit the business. In 1848 the company name was changed to David Roberts & Company in which David was partnered by William Jones. A further timber yard was opened in Fox Street and equipped with brand new machines to produce planks for the building trade. The Fox Street yard also became the company's headquarters.

By this time, roughly 1850, there were 70 timber companies in Liverpool, and many of them were owned by Welshmen. Of these, one of the most important was Walker & Roberts. And more timber companies were established by Welshmen in the 1860s, for example, John Hughes & Company and Isaac Evans & Company. But by far the most important of them all was David Roberts & Son.

The company grew further with the acquisition of a sawmill in Derby Road, Bootle. John Jones retired from the company in 1856 and a year later the eldest son John Roberts joined the company as an apprentice. Five years later, following the passing of William Jones in 1860, John became a partner. David Roberts had need of a partner, and he and his son were on good terms - more like two brothers that father and son. It was John Roberts who, in 1861, designed the new sawmill in Derby Road and it was he who named it the Cambrian Sawmills. When the site was bought by the Lancashire & Yorkshire Railway Company, John and his father decided to set up mills elsewhere, this time in Esk Street and Primrose Road in Bootle. In 1864 the company was joined by the son-in-law D. Lloyd Davies who served on the company Board until 1872. A further branch of the company was opened in Church Street, Birkenhead, its home until 1883 when it was moved to Bridge Street. Under John Roberts' leadership the company then, early in the 1860s, moved into the building trade and established a building empire that lasted until the 1930s.

We know very little about the mills or the timber yards themselves. However, we can guess at their scale from a description of a fire that occurred in 1879 at another Welsh company's yard, one well known to David Roberts, namely that of R. L. Lloyd on the corner of Dexter Street and Park Lane. The building had four stories, was 130 feet long, and contained within it a carpentry shop, sawing machinery, and a hall. to store the finished products . It took an hour and a half to bring the fire under control.

David Roberts was very proud of his good relationship with his workforce and by 1875 he had 400 people working for him in Liverpool and Birkenhead. During the summer, he and his son John would invite the whole workforce to spend a day with them in the grand new houses they had built for themselves in the town of Abergele.. He would boast that he had members of every denomination working for him in his sawmills and timber yards, and of both political parties of the time , in particular those that supported the Liberal and Conservative Parties..

3. David Roberts the Calvinist Methodist Elder. As we have seen, Bedford Street Chapel became David Roberts' spiritual home from the first week he arrived in Liverpool from Llanrwst . Bedford Street Welsh Calvinistic Methodist Chapel was bounded on all sides by chapels of the other denominations: the Welsh Independent chapel moved there from Greenland Street in 1838; the Welsh Wesleyan Methodist chapel came to Hill Street in 1833; and in 1829 the

Welsh Baptists started a chapel in Heath Street before moving to Stanhope Street in 1834. As the shipyards along the river grew so David Roberts saw Bedford Street Chapel also grow, for the shipyards employed many hundreds of workers, of whom a substantial number were Welsh speaking Welshmen. Indeed Bedford Street Chapel had to be rebuilt to cope with the new members that became active and enthusiastic members.. It was reopened on Good Friday April 9th, 1841. The arrival of the Reverend John Hughes (1796-1860) from the Wrexham area was of immense benefit to the Calvinist Methodist cause in Liverpool. He and his family became members of Bedford Street Chapel and great friends of David Roberts and his family, who were their neighbours in both Hope Street and Mount Street. John Hughes was a man of many talents. Between 1851 and 1855 he wrote three important volumes on the History of Welsh Calvinistic Methodism in Wales, volumes described by the renowned historian Dr R. T. Jenkins (also born in Toxteth, Liverpool) as indispensable for us at least one hundred years later. He was an important supporter of the famous preachers and scholars such Dr. Lewis Edwards, Principal of Bala Theological College and the Reverend Roger Edwards of Mold who had an awareness of the importance of politics for a religious denomination. Hughes was an influence on his famous and inspired saintly colleague, Reverend Henry Rees for they both came to Liverpool in the same year, 1836. He was also a great influence on David Roberts and his son John. It was no surprise that John later became his son-in-law.

David Roberts was elected elder for the first time in 1836, but because of doubts about the character of a certain William Williams of Frederick Street who also had been elected by the congregation , he persuaded the three other men who had been elected elders with him to stand down so as not to cause a rift in the congregation. Two years later, in March 1838, he was elected an elder for a second time. This time only he was elected, a real honour for him but the three that stood down in 1836 rather resented his interference.. He saw the chapel's membership grow from 480 in 1841 to 515 in 1856, then to 574 in 1860 and finally to 765 in 1865. The total membership, including full members, members on probation and children, had reached 952. David Roberts, working in perfect harmony with his minister the Reverend Dr David Saunders, was a key part of this growth as he persuaded many of his staff to join . When it was decided to build a new chapel in Princes Road , which became known as the Welsh Calvinistic Methodist Cathedral , the main motive force behind the whole project was David Roberts. He was chosen to preside over the Building Committee and within days had decided to build the new chapel on the broad boulevard then known as Princes Road. This was in the finest part of the city, and most of the land was also owned by David Roberts and his two sons. He had bought a large parcel of land there from Lord Sefton in the name of David Roberts & Son. Consequently he and his sons owned all the land around Parliament Fields, a large area leading up to Croxteth Road, Ullett Road and Smithdown Road. When he sold the land (to Welsh building companies) it was on condition that no tavern was to be built on any part of the estate. This made the Brooke House tavern for years and years the only one to be seen from Upper Parliament Street to Penny Lane. The design work for new chapel was entrusted to the architects Messrs. W & C Audsley who were also involved in the building of the handsome Synagogue in Princes Road.

A meeting was arranged to promote the new chapel on the 24th of January 1865 at Bedford Street Chapel. Hundreds came along to commit themselves and those assembled were astounded to hear David Roberts announce that the new chapel would cost £10,000 - equivalent to more than a million pounds in today's money (in actual fact, by the time the new chapel was finished, it was to cost nearly twice that amount). According to the Reverend Dr Owen Thomas (a future minister of the chapel in 1871) who wrote a most interesting biography of Henry Rees, the meeting was one of 'the most enthusiastic and successful meetings ever held in Liverpool'.

David Roberts was determined that the Welsh should show the city of Liverpool what an important contribution they had to make there in respect of architecture, religion, religious education and the preaching of the gospel. He himself embodied the Calvinistic ideal. Over a period of forty years the eighteen year old boy had, through God's will and the Protestant work ethic, become a successful, well thought Calvinis t millionaire. David Roberts sums it up in his sweeping statement: "When it comes to matters of religion, there is no such word as 'impossible' in the Welsh language." Among those enthused at that remarkable meeting was the Reverend Henry Rees, whose only daughter Anne was married to Richard Davies - another wealthy Welsh Calvinistic Methodist capitalist - of the Treborth estate near Bangor.

Chits were distributed among the audience for them to note the sum of money they wished to commit to this ambitious plan. This process took three quarters of an hour and Henry Rees took it upon himself to ask the Chairman, David Roberts, how much he intended to donate. David Roberts answered, quietly, that he 'was hoping to scrape together a four figure sum'. Henry Rees took from this that David Roberts intended to donate four hundred pounds. The actual amount David Roberts donated was an immense £1,272 pounds and 17 shillings, equivalent to roughly £120,000 of today's money. The second largest amount-£637 and 2 shillings - was donated by David Roberts' son, John. The next largest donation - £351 - was that of Thomas Davies, Berry Street. David Roberts also persuaded Lord Sefton to donate £200, and his neighbour John Lewis and his son-in-law D. Lloyd Davies the sum of £150 and 16 shillings. The historian J. Hughes Morris states: 'Never before had donations as generous as these been made to any of the   Welsh Calvinistic Methodists   causes. It is said that Mr David Roberts' donation of over a thousand pounds - a previously unheard of amount in a context such as this - was the reason for   more generous giving among the rank and file within the church.'

The foundation stone for Princes Road chapel was laid during the afternoon of Whit Monday, the 5th of June 1865. Only days previously 164 Welsh people had set off from Liverpool on the Mimosa boat to start a new life in Patagonia, a journey of eight thousand miles across the Atlantic to Argentina, yet more came to witness the laying of the new chapel's foundation stone than had been by the river Mersey to pay their farewell to the Mimosa and its   brave passengers. Today, ironically, Princes Road Chapel is a sad shadow of its former glory, while the Welsh people of Patagonia are flourishing, and opening Welsh language medium schools from the Gaiman to the Andes. Approximately three thousand people came to Princes Road that day, and were addressed by some of that period's greatest preachers: Dr Lewis Edwards of Bala;, David Saunders;Dr Owen Thomas, Henry Rees, and W. C. Roberts of New York. But who laid the stone? Who else but   the senior   Elder David Roberts. He was also presented with   a silver trowel bearing an inscription and a picture of the new chapel with the words: 'Presented by the young ladies of Bedford Street Chapel congregation to David Roberts esq. on the occasion of the laying by him of the foundation stone of Princes' Road Chapel, June 5th 1865.'

The total cost of the building work was £19,633 pounds, 8 shillings and fivepence. The additional £9, 000 plus pounds was a debt the chapel had to bear for a number of years after its official opening in 1868. This, according to the papers and magazines of the time, was both inside and outside   the most beautiful building in Liverpool and the surrounding region. It was a glorious achievement. Nowhere else, not in London or New York, in Patagonia or Australia, had the Welsh been as successful as they were in Liverpool. Not everyone was pleased with such splendour however and the opposition was led by Richard Jones of Gibson Street, a working class man and an eloquent speaker. His concern was with the stained-glass windows which, to him, smacked of Roman Catholicism. He was silenced in short order by David Roberts who stated that God and the Welsh people deserved nothing but the best. When Owen Thomas came as minister to the new chapel in 1871 he naturally became a regular visitor to 61 Hope Street, the Liverpool home of David and Jane Roberts.

On the Friday before Whitsun 1873 a further meeting was convened to deal with the debt, and garnered pledges of £4,400. Once again David Roberts contributed a thousand pounds - the only one to do so. His son, John, gave £500. It had been a cause of great joy to David Roberts to see John elected an Elder at Bedford Street in 1867, and the two of them shared many fruitful years working together in the administration of the chapel.

Lord Clwyd has recorded many valuable memories of his grandfather David Roberts, and of his religious activities at a time of great change in Welsh life, both in Wales itself and on Merseyside. His part in the religious life of Welsh people in Liverpool was an important aspect of his life. One of his projects was the establishment of the Presbyterian Foreign Mission Society following a meeting arranged by John Roberts known as Minimus, his brother-in-law, in the Vestry of Rose Place Welsh chapel on the 31st of January 1840 - a meeting presided over by the inspirational man of God Henry Rees. David Roberts was also active on behalf of, and generous towards, the Foreign Mission Society , which concentrated on India as well as Britany and he was was followed in this by his son. It was he, during a service in Mynydd Seion Welsh Calvinistic Methodist chapel in Abergele celebrating the fiftieth anniversary of the departure of Thomas Jones ,the first Welsh Calvinistic Methodist missionary to North East India. John Roberts spoke of the need to establish a theological college in the province of Khasia and a new mission to the area known then as Sylhet, and for essential medical work throughout the Bhoi villages. A collection was made and the sum of £165 was collected. Of this £100 was donated by John Roberts, £50 by his son J. Herbert Roberts and the remaining £15 was donated by the congregation. Without the Roberts family the congregation would have been struggling.!

David Roberts was also a leading light in the field of higher education. He was of the same mind as his contemporary, Sir Hugh Owen (1804-1881) of London, and the two did a great deal of work together. In 1865 David Roberts, Hugh Owen and the Reverend John Phillips (1810-1867) were sponsors of the movement to establish an educational institution known as the Normal College in Bangor - for the purposes of training teachers to teach in British schools in Britain and abroad - and it was these three talented men that were mainly responsible for the establishment of the College. The Normal College was essentially a Welsh Calvinistic Methodist College and it cost £13,000 to build. Only £2,000 was forthcoming from the British government and John Phillips and David Roberts were the men who raised the remaining £11,000. David Roberts was also the main sponsor of the Theological College established in the town of Bala to educate as well as train young men for Christian Ministry in the Connexion. The main motivator for this project was John Elias of Anglesey, a regular worshipper at Bedford Street Chapel, whose second wife, Lady Bulkeley, the widow of Sir John Bulkeley of Presaddfed, Anglesey, was a chapel member for a few years. David Roberts and John Elias became acquaintances to the extent that David Roberts was present at John Elias' wedding to Lady Bulkeley at Saint David's Welsh Anglican Church in Liverpool in Russell Street on the 10th of February 1830. It is no surprise that the Reverend Lewis Edwards, the principal of the college in Bala, came so readily to preach at Bedford Street Chapel given that this was the chapel of his most important financial supporter, David Roberts.

David Roberts thought the world of every aspect of the work of Bedford Street Chapel and later of Princes Road Chapel. On 6th August 1869, at David Roberts' invitation, the five hundred members of Princes Road Sunday school in Liverpool came all the way by train to Abergele. They came with their teachers on the train and were led by a brass band from the station and through the town to the then new Presbyterian chapel of Mynydd Seion (Mount Zion). There they were addressed by Peter Williams of Liverpool, a successful clothing merchant who had made a fortune since he left Brymbo as a young lad. He and David Roberts were best friends; the gravestone of Williams in Smithdown cemetery is the tallest by far and a monument to his apparent worldly success. The other speaker that day was the Reverend R. Roberts of Brynhyfryd. Following this official welcome there was another procession, this time to Tan yr Allt, David Roberts' home in Abergele. There a splendid marquee had been provided and within it a sumptuous meal for the five hundred. And there also to welcome them were David Roberts and his family, and his son's family from their home in Abergele, Bryngwenallt. No expense was spared. After the meal there was a walk through the gardens of Tan yr Allt, then through the grounds of Bryngwenallt and out into the countryside towards Llanfair Talhaearn. Everybody then returned to the marquee where afternoon tea of cakes and other delicacies had been laid out for them. During tea, the leader of the Liverpool welsh Church, the Reverend Owen Thomas, thanked the Roberts family for their generosity. During his time as minister at Princes

Road, the Reverend Owen Thomas was a frequent guest at Tan yr Allt and Bryngwenallt. He loved it there when he needed rest from his strenuous ministry in Liverpool and as a preacher who travelled all over Wales

Bryngwenallt, Abergele

The local newspaper describes the event in the following words: 'They [the Princes Road members] were dignified and noble of appearance. We have, from time to time, been witness to numerous visits of this kind, but never did we see such a large number of such respectable people in apperance The numerous and respectable members left Tan yr Allt at 5.30 that evening in order to catch the 6.15 train back to Liverpool. '' The following afternoon the local Sunday School from Mynydd Seion was invited to Tan yr Allt for tea in the marquee.

Lord Clwyd writes with fondness about his grandfather as a religious man. He describes him as the one who led the family prayers, and the one who presided over the daily family observance both in Hope Street and Abergele. He describes also his contribution to the Sunday evening Society meeting where his observations would raise the congregation to a higher plane. And the hymn he would ask them to sing would always be:

Braint, braint
yw cael cymdeithas gyda'r saint,
na welodd neb erioed ei maint:
ni ddaw un haint iddynt hwy;
 y mae'r gymdeithas yma'n gref,
ond yn y nef hi fydd yn fwy.

[It is a privilege, a privilege
To be in society with the saints
A society whose extent no-one has ever witnessed:
They shall suffer no infection.
This society is strong,
But in heaven it will be stronger still.]

Lord Clwyd recalls also his grandfather's gifted leadership of the Seiat (Society
) , an unique religious meeting [where people bore witness to their daily
experience of life with God], a spiritual meeting held every week that none of us
these days will have experienced. Dr. Owen Thomas would call often upon
David Roberts to help him, saying, for example:
'Mr David Roberts, would you be so good as to take the floor for a few
minutes? I see …. over there, Mr …... He has been unwell. Please   converse
with him for a while ' And then:
'And behind him is   Mr …. He recently lost a son. Please give him a few
words of comfort.'
And David Roberts would attend to the given tasks during the last half hour of
the meeting. Then the   minister Dr Owen Thomas , the historian and
theologian would take over and regularly spend another session. At least an
hour and a half would be spent weekly in a Society meeting at Princes Road
church.

 David Roberts m had a tremendous love for and knowledge of the hymns of
William Williams (1717-1791) of Pantycelyn, one of the giants of the
eighteenth century Methodist Revival, and also of his poems to men and
women thart he knew as an itinerant evangelist. He also took a leading role in
the establishment of English Presbyterian chapels, and it was he and his son
who paid for the construction of Pensarn Chapel near Abergele before
presenting it to the North Wales Presbyterian Association in 1879; he was a
Welshman of conviction, but he was also concerned about the fate of the
nation's non-Welsh speakers.

He took on responsibilities with the Home Mission Society, not only   with the
English language   chapels, the Ministers' Fund, and the Peoples' Society.
When David Davies of Mount Gardens , Liverpool died in 1860, David Roberts
was appointed trustee to the Foreign Overseas Mission and treasurer for the
fund for missionaries, widows and orphans in need of care in Assam. When he
took over, the fund had £1,000 at its disposal. When he died, this sum had
grown to over £49,000.

A testimonial fund was established in his honour and the sum collected was
presented to him at his home in Hope Street on 9th March 1886 by sixteen
men of distinction in north Wales and Liverpool. These were led by his minister
Dr Owen Thomas and Dr John Hughes (1827-1893), a native of Anglesey and
a minister in Liverpool since 1856 and another frequent visitor to Hope Street.

He was also presented with a portrait of himself and paintings of Princes Road, Mynydd Seion and Pensarn chapels, of the Normal College in Bangor and of Tan yr Allt. The frame was four feet six inches tall by three feet and gilded. The paintings entrepreneur was signed by noted and wealthy Calvinistic Methodist elders , among them Edward Davies, the only son of the entrepeneur David Davies (1818-1890) of Llandinam, Montgomeryshire , a railway and coal mining pioneer. David Roberts was in good health that day and thoroughly enjoyed the occasion.

Within six months however he had passed to glory, passing away during the night of Sunday 3rd October 1886; he had always wanted to pass away on the Sabbath. He had attended his last chapel service on the last Sunday of August that year. It is worth remembering that by then he had been an Elder in Liverpool for 50 years and in Abergele for 30 years. The funeral was organised over two days. The first day was to be in Abergele that is on Thursday October the 7th. It began with the mourners walking from Tan yr Allt to Mynydd Seion Chapel singing the hymn that starts:

'Mae 'nghyfeillion adre'n myned
O fy mlaen o un i un'

[*My friends are going home*
Before me one by one.]

and also the hymn:

'Bydd myrdd o ryfeddodau ar doriad bore wawr.'

[*A host of wondrous things will happen at the dawning of the day.*]

There were five eulogies and fifteen hundred people present, among them Reverend R.A.Jones known as Emrys ap Iwan, the father of modern Welsh devolution. Every shop and business in Abergele was closed and all the curtains drawn. The coffin was carried to the chapel, and then from the chapel to the train station, by workers from Tan yr Allt and Bryngwenallt. It was then put on the 4 o'clock train to Liverpool to be ready in time for the following day's service. On that Friday an estimated five thousand of Liverpool's residents came to the funeral. The family was taken from Hope Street to Princes Road in five carriages. The chapel that would not have existed were it not for David Roberts was full to overflowing and there were thousands outside. The congregation was addressed by Dr. Owen Thomas, by Thomas Levi (1825- 1916) the minister of Tabernacl church in Aberystwyth and editor of 'Trysorfa'r Plant' (The Children's Treasury – the magazine for children printed in easily read language and which sold 40,000 copies every month), by Francis Jones, David Roberts' minister in Abergele, and Dr. John Hughes of Liverpool. Present also were: the Reverend Daniel Rowlands (1827-1917) Principal of the Normal College, Bangor; Professor Hugh Williams (1843-1911), the professor of Greek and Mathematics at the College in Bala; Professor Ellis Edwards (1844-1915), professor of Latin, Greek and English at the same college, and son of the Reverend Roger Edwards of Mold; Professor Henry Jones (1852-1922), then professor of Philosophy at the University College of North Wales, Bangor; the Reverend William James (1833-1905), minister of Moss Side Calvinistic Methodist Chapel in Manchester and a major figure in the North Wales Association; and his doctor, Dr Gee of Abercrombie Square. There was also one MP present, namely J. Bryn Roberts. There were many male mourners including David Roberts' son, John, his sons-in-law, his brother Robert Roberts and his seven grandchildren. There were carriages representing the timber trade, elders from both north and south Wales Presbyterian Asssociations, and dignitaries from Liverpool City Council. The coffin was made of polished oak. Walking from Princes Road to Saint James cemetery were ministers, the Princes Road Chapel Elders, and individuals representing the Sunday Schools, chapel societies and public institutions among the large Liverpool Welsh community.

The lad from Llanrwst had succeeded in becoming one of the greatest businessmen in Liverpool and in doing so had made the best of both worlds. At the same time, as noted in the 'Goleuad' (the Presbyterian weekly newspaper) of 16th October 1886, he was 'a good man, a man of God, and a man of the people'. David Roberts was a man of lively and perceptive intelligence, warm, quick natured and also, at times, excitable. But the foundation of his great character was his Presbyterian faith. Dr. Owen Thomas' message to his mourners was 'be like David Roberts'. In his last will and testament (dated 4th March 1886) he left the sum of sixty thousand, six hundred and ninety eight pounds, one shilling and sevenpence, the equivalent today of approximately £650,000. The executors were his son John Roberts and his grandson John Henry Roberts. To his daughter Elizabeth Anne Henry, wife of the Reverend Henry Jones Henry, he left a tea and coffee set of best silver, and a sum of £3,000, and to Mary Robinson, the niece of his late wife, £100. Elizabeth Anne

Henry and his other daughter Jane Lloyd Jones and their families were left £22,000 between them and a sum of £28,000 to invest. The remainder was left to John his son and Member of Parliament..

4. John Roberts, the businessman, politician and Elder of the Church..

John Roberts the eldest son was born in Liverpool in 1835 into a thoroughly Presbyterian household. Like his father, he made a second home of Bedford Street Chapel, and also like his father, his grandfather Richard Roberts, his uncle Minimus and his father-in-law John Hughes of the Mount, he became a religious leader. He was educated at Liverpool Institute and then sent away, as was Winston Churchill, to a private school in Brighton. He was extremely talented, particularly in mathematics, and should really have had the opportunity to study at Oxford or Cambridge. But his father had need of his help with the timber business which was growing at a tremendous rate.

While he was in Brighton John was able to attend Trinity Chapel where the unforgettable Frederick William Robertson (1816-1853), known as Robertson of Brighton, was preacher. Robertson achieved great fame, in spite of his early death at 37 years of age.John met his future wife, Katherine Tudor Hughes, at a literary meeting in Bedford Street Welsh Calvinistic Methodist Chapel. She was the daughter of the Reverend and Mrs John Hughes of Mount Street. The two married and set up home at 63 Hope Street, close by both sets of parents. Unlike his father, John took an active interest in politics, and in the politics of the Liberal Party particularly. The Liberals, whose leaders were wealthy and mostly Anglicans or Unitarians, weren't as active in Liverpool as they should have been and as they were in Wales. But among their number were men like William Rathbone the Fifth (1787-1867), the humanitarian and reformer. He caused outrage at the City Council in 1820 when - in accordance with Quaker custom - he didn't remove his hat when the Council leader was conducting a minute's silence to mark the death of King George the Fourth. The hat was knocked off his head by an aggressive Tory councillor , and immediately William Rathbone responded and on his feet in the Town Hall reminded everyone in the chamber that freedom of expression was a human right that should not be so easily cast away. By 1837 he was Mayor of Liverpool, but it is clear that the Liverpool Liberalism of the time was not as radical as the Rathbone family or even of John Roberts. Roberts naturally , was drawn to the condition of his own Dissenting people in Wales and the need for material improvement.

John Roberts was obviously a product of his people's religion - in his case Welsh Presbyterianism or Welsh Calvinistic Methodism as experienced among the Welsh exiles of Liverpool and later the Welsh of Abergele - and not of social clubs like so many of Liverpoool Liberals as well as humanitarian societies. 'The chapels,' writes the historian Ieuan Gwynedd Jones, 'in creating their own values, produced men who embodied those values, and so created their own *élite*.' And there was no-one who better represented that *élite* than John Hughes, David Roberts, Owen and John Thomas, Roger Edwards and Lewis Edwards. They were the first of a new urbane dynasty, in particular a nonconformist dynasty. After all, Wales was a much more religious in practise and activities than even Liverpool with its large Irish influx . The majority would be Roman Catholics expect for the Presbyterians of the North many with Orange Day involvement but in politics the religious Irish had many allegiances ; you will recall that David Roberts was the product of the Beddgelert Revival and that he and his son also witnessed the 1859 revival. This Revival increased chapel membership tremendously, including that of Bedford Street, and John Roberts was determined to act for his fellow Christians. He became one of the main founders of the Welsh Reform Association, and spoke with great influence at that memorable meeting of May 1868 in the Liverpool Amphitheatre. The main speaker was the educator John Bright, but the name on everyone's lips was that of John Roberts, and it was his presence that drew the meeting's capacity crowd. Bright and the others there saw the potential in this young thirty three year old man and soon afterwards John Roberts was appointed Magistrate in Liverpool and then in Denbighshire as well , for his father, remember, had secured a second home in Abergele since the middle 1850s. That year John Roberts was a proposer of George Osborne Morgan (1826-1897) as one of the two MPs to represent Denbighshire in Parliament; the other was Sir Watkin Williams-Wynn. George Osborne Morgan was a good example of a Liberal politician for John Roberts, for his priorities were measures concerned with Welsh religious non-conformism. For example, in 1870, as a result of what had happened the previous year at the Menai Bridge funeral of the Reverend Henry Rees of Liverpool, he proposed a measure that would permit any Christian denomination to hold services in parish graveyards. He had to propose it ten times in all in the House of Commons before succeeding to have it put into the law of the land in 1880.

Between 1870 and 1878, John Roberts' name was mentioned repeatedly as that of a possible parliamentary candidate. Then, on the 3rd of July 1878, he was given his opportunity. It was not going to be easy, however. There was another contender , a certain E. K. Muspratt, an accomplished speaker whose home was

Trelawney House, Flint, who had his eye on the Flint Borough seat. But in the end it was John Roberts who was selected to fight the by-election. The seat encompassed seven towns: Flint, Overton, Holywell, Caerwys, Mold, Caergwrle and St Asaph. The seat had become vacant as a result of the death of Ellis Eyton, its MP since 1874. John Roberts' opponent, Phillip Pennant Pennant, was from a well-known family, and the Tories had strong support in a number of places - particularly in Britain's smallest town, St Asaph, but also in Overton. John Roberts won the election with a majority of 125.

As a man of the chapel, John Roberts was well aware of the passion of nonconformists of every denomination for the sanctification of the Sabbath as a day for worship and education. The only places open in Wales on a Sunday were the chapel and the tavern. Even the train from Merthyr to Cardiff didn't run on a Sunday. As one old hand was noted to say: 'The great ones of the country had got rich by the labour of the working classes, and they grudged them the little relaxation which a Sunday trip gave them.' 77% of north Wales taxpayers were in favour of the Sunday closing of taverns. Indeed, 793 of the taverns themselves signed in favour of closing, with only 153 expressing opposition.

In September 1879 John Roberts laid before Parliament a measure for the Sunday closing of taverns in Wales. The measure was first read on February 6th 1880 and supported by Henry Richards the Apostle of Peace, by Samuel Holland Member for Merionethshire, Henry Vivian Member for Glamorgan, and both Members for Denbighshire, Watkin Williams-Wynn and Osborne Morgan. In his speech in support of the second reading on the 30th of June, John Roberts referred to the Irish Sunday closing law that had been passed in 1878. All the Welsh MPs were in favour of the measure; tavern owners could count no friends among them and had to have the support of the MP for Bridport, Edward Warton, to oppose the measure on their behalf. He made a very poor case, particularly given that the basis of his argument was that Wales was merely another part of England. The measure passed its second reading without a division of the House and by July 1880 had passed to Committee for further scrutiny. It took until 1881 for the measure to secure the support necessary for it to pass into Law, with only Lord Emlyn of Carmarthen opposing it. The argument for the measure was summed up perfectly by Osborne Morgan: 'I think it is time that people should understand that in dealing with Wales you are really dealing with an entirely distinct nationality, a nationality more distinct than that of the Scotch or Irish, because Wales is separated from England not merely by race and by geographical boundaries, but by a barrier which interposes at every turn of life - I mean the barrier of language.' The campaign however was successful, and that partly because William Gladstone, the then Prime Minister, spoke for a quarter of an hour in favour of the measure. The measure was passed with a majority of 147. Only 17 voted against.

John Roberts had to contest another election in 1880, during which he and his wife canvassed from an open carriage. He won again against Philip Pennant Pennant and the result was as follows:

John Roberts (Liberal) - 2,039 votes
P. P. Pennant (Conservative) - 1,468 votes
Majority   - 571 votes

According to the Cambrian News the whole population of Abergele turned out to welcome John Roberts from the train from Flint. There was much singing, in both languages, during the campaign. Here is an example of one of the English verses:

Pennant, like Brutus, may honourable be,
But he's not the man to be Flintshire's MP. So work
boys for Roberts the friend of working men, And
never rest contented 'til you have him up again.

And one in Welsh:

Mae'n nefoedd Ryddfrydol yn bloeddio'n gytun,
Ro'wch Pennant i gadw, John Roberts yw'r dyn.
[*The Liberal heaven proclaims in unison*
Put Pennant aside, Roberts is the man.]

On 13th September 1880 Katherine Tudor, John Roberts' wife, died at the early age of 43 years of age. This was a great loss, for many reasons. She had been at his side at every meeting, in every one of the seven towns, speaking herself with voters and always friendly and always kind. She had spent the end of July and August of that summer of 1880 at Bryngwenallt in the company of her children. On the 2nd of September she went to her room and the following day gave birth to their twelfth child, Cecil. (The couple had lost two of their children, Mary Ellen and Gladys to scarlet fever.) She had persuaded John Herbert and Trevor his brother to take a holiday in the Lake District with friends from Princes Road

Chapel, Harrison Jones, J. C. Evans, and an uncle. They rented a cottage in
Clappergate and on the 18th of September had a wonderful day climbing
Helvellyn. On their return to the cottage they found the owner, Miss Allenby,
waiting for them with what was then called a red letter, namely a telegram. On
opening the telegram they learnt of their mother's death. On their return to
Abergele they were met by David Roberts. At this point John Herbert Roberts'
account comes to an end, and one can understand why, for he had lost his
mother and one who had taken great care of him. Dr. Owen Thomas was asked
to make the arrangements for the funeral and in this was aided by his brother,
the Reverend Dr. John Thomas, minister of a Welsh Independent chapel in
Liverpool. Among the non-family mourners was Richard Davies, MP for
Anglesey, and other members of the affluent Treborth family.

John Roberts had three homes, one at 67 Lancaster Gate, Hyde Park, London,
the one in Hope Street, Liverpool and Bryngwenallt in Abergele. And keeping
his seat in Flintshire was no easy task, in spite of his skill and hard work. After
his father passed away he ran the business in Liverpool with his brother and
encouraged his son John Herbert to pursue a career in politics. His kindness
and concern for his workers and for the poor people of Liverpool and Abergele
were limitless. He worked hard for the Presbyterian English Cause Fund (for
the establishment of English chapels) in north Wales and was its
Treasurer. He ensured that there was always 'Calennig' (New Year's day, good
luck, gift) for the poor people of Abergele. This would be a packet of tea,
sixpence and an orange for every child that called to see them on New Year's
Day, On that day in 1894 he gave out a thousand quarter pound packets of tea.

Pennant stood against him for a third time in the 1885 election, a particularly
difficult one for John Roberts as he no longer had his wife at his side to
campaign with him. He won, but with a reduced majority of 123 votes.

John Roberts (Liberal)   - 1,835 votes
P. P. Pennant (Conservative)   - 1,713 votes
Majority   - 123 votes

A year later John Roberts had to stand for election again, though not against
Phillip Pennant this time, who did not stand. The Liberal Party was divided over
the question of Irish Home Rule and this time it was another Liberal, Sir H. M.
Jackson, who opposed him, standing as a Liberal Unionist. John Roberts won
again, this time with an increased majority.

John Roberts (Liberal)   - 1,827 votes
Sir H. M. Jackson (Liberal Unionist) - 1,403 votes
Majority   - 424 votes

He was known for being a politician who spoke well and would give a good account of his stewardship wherever he was. He was the only MP who visited every one of the constituency's towns to report on his work. And as MP he received strong support from non-conformist ministers such as the Reverends David Oliver of Holywell, D. M. Jenkins and Josiah Thomas of the Liverpool Welsh community. Another of his famous supporters was the preacher and novelist Daniel Owen of Mold , author of best selling novels 'Rhys Lewis' and 'Enoc Huws'. In 1889 he spent two months in the United States of America, travelling with his son John Herbert. On his return he travelled throughout the constituency speaking about his impressions of the great land across the sea whose port of New York was three weeks voyage away.

In 1891, after 13 years of service to the Liberal Party and the Temperance Movement, John Roberts decided to give up his constituency; his health was no longer what it had been. It was a source of great joy to him, however, to hand over the reins to John Herbert Lewis (1858-1933), a Liverpool lawyer and in 1889, the first Chair of Flintshire County Council. J. H. Lewis was a Flintshire man from Mostyn, a grand-nephew of the theologian Thomas Jones of Denbigh. He served as MP for Flintshire from 1892 to 1906.

John Roberts' life ended suddenly and unexpectedly on the evening of Saturday the 24th of February 1894. He was at West Dingle in Liverpool and had been unwell for some time. The funeral was not held in Liverpool as was his father's, but rather in Abergele where he was laid to rest with his wife. He had made his will on the 29th of November 1892 and his personal estate was valued at one hundred and sixty three thousand, three hundred and ninety five pounds, six shillings and ninepence. The executors for his estate were his sons, John Herbert Roberts MP and David Trevor Roberts of West Dingle. John Herbert was bequeathed a sum of £40,000 along with pictures, dishes, furniture, household goods, and the horses and carriages. David Trevor was bequeathed the sum of ten thousand pounds. It had been John Roberts' intention to divide the remainder in equal shares among his other children, with the exception that John Herbert's share was to be twice that of the other six sons and two daughters. It is interesting to note here that a sum of a thousand pounds was given to his son Arthur Lloyd Roberts of the Louisianna Sugar Company in the United States of America.

Even though John Roberts himself had passed away, the dynasty continued. David Trevor Roberts took charge of David Roberts & Co. after John Herbert was elected MP, and ushered in a further golden age for the company in the 20th century. And the company's motto, the unofficial motto of Liverpool builders, was maintained: 'Justice from Owen Elias (the 'king' of the Liverpool building trade) and mercy from David Roberts & Co, all benefactors ardent in their morality, temperance and Christianity.' These two remarkable men, father and son , have been neglected for much too long . At last we have through the Merseyside Welsh Heritage Society have rectified this neglect and I am glad that I had the opportunity to research their lives and contribution to nineteenth century Liverpool and Wales.

A brief bibliography

(i) In Welsh

a) **Lewis Edwards** (D. Densil Morgan, Cyfres Dawn Dweud, Cardiff, 2009)

b) **Hanes Methodistiaeth Calfinaidd Cymru, Cyfrol 3, 'Y Twf a'r Cadarnhau 1814-1914** (John Gwynfor Jones a Marian Beech Hughes (Golygyddion), Caernarfon 2011)

c) **Hanes Methodistiaeth Liverpool, Cyfrol 1** (J. Hughes Morris, Liverpool 1929)

ch) **Pregethwr y Bobl: Bywyd a Gwaith Owen Thomas** (D. Ben Rees, Cyhoeddiadau Modern, Liverpool and Pontypridd, 1979)

(ii) In English

a) **Building the Industrial City** (Martin Doughty, Leicester, 1986)

b) **The Welsh Builder on Merseyside** (J. R. Jones, Liverpool 1946)

c) **Memoirs by Lord Clwyd** (John Herbert Roberts, privately printed, Abergele, 1937)

d) **Local and Parliamentary Politics in Liverpool from 1800 to 1911, Studies in British History, Volume 55** (D. Ben Rees, Lewiston, Queenston, Lampeter, 1999)

David Roberts' Descendants including David Trevor Roberts and John Herbert Roberts, Lord Clwyd 1863-1955
By Lawrence Holden

John Herbert Roberts had much to live up to. He was the eldest of twelve
children of inspiring parents. He had one exceptionally able grandfather and
another deeply spiritual grandfather. His father John had stepped into his
father's mantle and, with great energy, made his mark on history and established
a sizeable fortune. Both David and John had warm and close relationships with
Herbert. They both made his responsibility and his destiny quite clear. All this
put expectations and pressure on a thoughtful man. In looking at his life there
are signs of a complex and enigmatic character who always strove hard to do the
right thing. He certainly had a sense of public responsibility.

Herbert had a double inheritance, of wealth certainly, but also of responsibility
towards Welsh cultural ideals and resurgence. By the time of his death he was a
highly respected figure, known for a host of public work and private generosity.
He was devout in his Welsh Calvinistic Methodist beliefs and retained,
throughout his long life, a deep faith in the Welsh Spiritual revival and the

social change this demanded. He had a great belief in Liberal principles and values.

Herbert Roberts was one of four "family" Liberal MPs along with his father John Roberts, his father-in-law William Sproston Caine and his wife's brotherin-law Herbert Lewis. The period 1892 -1914 was a momentous one for the Liberal cause in Wales. It is a fascinating period to study and there are many resonances with contemporary problems despite the vast changes that have taken place. To understand the lives of these notable family members we need to do a bit of time travelling, because life in Wales in those days was so utterly different from our complex society.

In his memoir, written in 1937, Herbert Roberts recalls "the essential importance of the spiritual revival of 200 years ago, which gave birth to our Denomination and which was followed by later religious awakenings which left a deep mark upon the development of our national life". In the nineteenth century preachers and politicians could and did frequently draw crowds of thousands. There was much travelling despite the lack of motorcars. By any independent analysis Wales was a land with a grievously suppressed majority. This manifested itself in religious, educational, cultural, economic and land ownership terms. A traveller in 1854 found Wales "an unfamiliar land, alien in speech and primitive in customs".

The parliamentary Reform Acts of 1867 and 1884 were genuinely empowering but the journey was hard, contentious and complicated by English and Irish politics. The population of Wales grew over the nineteenth century from 587,000 in 1801 to over 2 million in 1901 and there was also large-scale migration out of Wales and to the new centres of industry. At least a quarter of the population was non- conformist and the chapel was the centre of life for most people with Sunday Schools in Chapels being a crucial source of education. As late as 1879 there were less than 4,000 pupils in secondary education in Wales. The ignorance of the English about Welsh culture was offensive. One significant episode of the notorious "blue books" written by three Commissioners examining the Welsh educational situation in 1847 actually triggered a flowering of expression of Welsh culture. Vexatious evictions of farmers were another grievous source of gross unfairness. The situation was not simple and varied from area to area but these are indications of the context in which the religious spirit, which inspired so many members of the family, was born. It was a matter of creating the essential freedom in which a wonderful culture and faith could find full expression and flourish. It was to be a culture of self-improvement.

In his obituary of Lord Clwyd, an astute Welsh academic administrator, Sir Wynn Wheldon, ended with the question "How could any young man be better ushered into public life in Denbighshire than the youthful John Herbert Roberts in the late 1880s?" The question was a tribute to his grandfather and parents; the answer is clearly that the inheritance described was a bountiful one but in order to give more than a superficial understanding of what he made of this opportunity and his life we will need to probe important new influences of his early adulthood. Travel and a deep interest in India brought him into contact with Sproston Caine, an outstanding character, described by political associates as a "genial ruffian" and his cultured, fascinating family, and led to his deep love with his daughter Hannah who became his wife. It also led to his friend Herbert Lewis being brought into the family circle with four Liberal MPs when Hannah's sister Ruth and Herbert Lewis fell in love at first sight. The combined Caine and Lewis family became one of the most stimulating radical families of the time. They were also very effective in practical terms and got things done.

Herbert Robert's thinking received a severe jolt in 1885, when he was 22. His father, feeling a decline in strength and health, took him to the Lake District (curiously far from Wales!) and, near the Langdale Pikes, announced his decision not to stand at the next General Election and told him that he must stand in his place. This was certainly a life changing moment. In his memoir Herbert wrote that at the time he did not personally desire Parliamentary life.

Five years before that jolt, again in the Lake District, he had suffered a severe shock on receiving a "red paper" telling him of the death of his much loved mother who had influenced him deeply. She thought to give him and his brother Trevor some pleasure by sending them to the Lake District for her 12th confinement. She was not to know that she would die after giving birth to their youngest brother Cecil. He wrote that the death of his mother placed him, as eldest son, in a position of special responsibility and it is clear that he took this very seriously.

A year later, having been educated at home by his mother and tutors, he experienced the "delight" in occupying rooms at Trinity College Cambridge which he recorded as " opening the door to a new world bringing with it a wider outlook and a fuller knowledge of men and things". His horizons were broadening. His experiences at Cambridge were followed by an intensive tour of the world with two rather special friends for just over a year from July 1894. The friends were Herbert Lewis and Henry Rees Davies son of a Richard Davies MP a Welsh ship-owner and non-conformist politician who was a colleague at Trinity College. They were both to remain lifelong friends. Herbert Lewis was to become a member of the reforming 1906 Cabinet and is rated one of the most effective Welsh Liberals in creating distinctively Welsh institutions. He was five years older than Herbert Roberts, much travelled and educated at Montreal and Oxford and deeply embedded in Welsh idealism.

The world tour was made in some style. The travels were far removed from a contemporary graduation-backpacking affair. It was carefully planned, with many letters of introduction, the best hotels, a magnificent dinner in Government House, Madras and many other notable meetings with leading local people, a major visit to the Welsh Missionary work in the Khasi Hills of Assam and other visits to Christian educationalists and missionaries. Superficially the three might have appeared to be upper class rich young men but in their minds they were serious, enquiring and radical thinkers with strong individual sense of personal responsibility. They really wished to scrutinise the influences of Christianity, methods of government and social issues and problems. In Herbert's enquiring mind the twin issues of temperance and how India was governed loomed large and became lifelong concerns.

Sproston Caine also made a world tour three years after the trio and formed similar views although he expressed them in much blunter terms. He was moved to action and formed the Anglo-Indian Temperance Society. Naturally Herbert Roberts was drawn to this Society. Rapidly he and Sproston Caine became close collaborators. There is no doubt whatsoever that Herbert fell deeply in love with Hannah, describing his marriage as "the greatest privilege of my life". Events moved quickly. Hannah watched his maiden speech in the Commons in March 1893 and they were married on 1st August. Caine was and avid art collector and owned three paintings by George Clausen. He commissioned Clausen to paint Hannah and the result is a work of beautiful simplicity. It is now in the Walker Art Gallery having been donated by the family. The friendship with Clausen continued and a strong family interest in art was established.

Sproston Caine, MP

The Caine connection was full of liveliness. Sproston Caine's father Nathaniel was a metal merchant, a member of the Wesleyan Methodist Church whose integrity brought him some highly advantageous deals. His mother was the daughter of William Rushton a local leader of the anti-slavery movement. As a child he was full of life, fun and mischief. He started his business career at the White Star Line at the age of fourteen. At the age of eighteen he was attracted by a young merchant preacher WP Lockhart and was "converted" to preaching himself. His father commented, "Whatever William does he over-does". At the age of nineteen he became a commercial traveller in his father's business and was deeply influenced by Rev Hugh Stowell Brown, a renowned preacher and social reformer whose statue now stands proudly opposite the Philharmonic Hall and who was much loved by Liverpool people. Caine conducted services and, assisted by his sister, became superintendent of the little Sunday school. This brought the Caine and Brown families very close and Sproston Caine married Alice Stowell Brown, the daughter of Hugh on 24th March 1868, and his sister Phoebe became the second wife of Stowell Brown.

Sproston and Alice had five children and they grew up amidst much art and creativity with many visitors of diverse and challenging opinions. Both Hannah and Ruth had upbringings that served them well as the wives of Welsh Liberal MPs although they were very different in character. Dorothea was exceptional. William qualified as a Barrister but had a career as an illustrator and author whilst tragedy struck David whilst climbing the awesome Napes Needle at Wastwater in April 1908.

Herbert Lewis had a very happy first marriage to Adelaide Hughes who died prematurely in 1895. Hannah and Herbert invited him to Bryngwenallt in one Sunday in 1896.and there was love at first sight. Ruth had been to Cambridge was radical (to the point of having republican views) and musical. They married in August 1897 and it was a most fulfilling union. Sproston Caine was dubbed "the father-in-law of the House". In reality the spirit, attitudes and culture that the Caine influence brought to the vital group of Welsh Liberal MPs can only have assisted and fortified their journey to becoming the great reforming government of 1906.

During the seven-year period from 1885 when he accepted his father's wish that he become an MP to 1892, when he was first elected, Herbert worked hard but also followed the new influences whilst building on his father's political direction.

Hannah later Lady Clwyd

The wealth was considerable. Building on the successful timber business of David Roberts, his father had advanced the land development business as well as pursuing his radical political career. The Architect and Surveyor with whom he worked so constructively, Richard Owens referred to Messrs D Roberts and Sons as "the largest land speculators in Liverpool". This development was certainly driven by a confident understanding of the needs of the Welsh community. The development brought profit and served the Liverpool Welsh community in several ways. It created a form of housing that matched their needs. It has been regarded with considerable affection to this day as it had integrity in the detail of its design and layout. It provided employment for the high proportion of the Welsh community that had building skills. In May 1890 Sproston Caine MP, was able to explain in the House of Commons how the prohibition of Public Houses on the Roberts development also added value. In his personal housing John Roberts did not refrain from flaunting his wealth. Both West Dingle his home in Liverpool and Bryngwenallt, designed by Richard Owens and built adjoining Tanyrallt (acquired by his father David) were exotic. This taste in architecture was something considered proper within the Calvinistic Welsh community as they, after due deliberation chose the renowned Audsley Brothers to design their new grand chapel in Princes Road.

At the time of his early death at the age of 58 in February 1894 John's estate was sworn at £163,562. Using the Bank of England inflation calculator that is over £19 million today. The Executors were Herbert and his brother Trevor. John and Catherine had 12 children in all but John's Will has a very strong element of primogeniture with the result that Herbert had a considerable inheritance.

Herbert inherited all his father's Welsh property, a legacy of £40,000 and a double share of the residue inherited by all his children. Trevor received a legacy of £10,000. There were special provisions relating to his building estates and properties and this explains why so many Liverpool people live in houses where the sale of alcohol was prohibited under covenants imposed by John Herbert Roberts and David Trevor Roberts. Inheritance Tax was actually introduced in 1894 so in John's case there would only have been a relatively low tax on each inheritor. Hence Herbert would have an inheritance of about £7 million in today's money. He could afford to be independent minded, be generous and live in some style both at Bryngwenallt and in London.

Herbert followed his father's instruction and became busy on the political scene both in Denbighshire and in London, but was very fortunate that his very able younger brother Trevor supported him loyally in the family business in Liverpool. According to Ellen, the elder daughter of Herbert's sister Meiwen, Trevor was the "brains" of the family. He obtained first class honours in the Law Tripos at Trinity College Cambridge and became a barrister in Liverpool. In his memoir Herbert included a fulsome tribute to his brother Trevor. Recording "his deep sense of obligation to him for his constant consideration and for innumerable deeds of kindness to myself and to members of my family. He gave up his career at the Bar in order to undertake the responsibilities of our business in Liverpool and thus to enable me to enter Parliament. His outstanding qualities both of mind and of heart, are known to you and I shall always treasure with gratitude the memory of his great contribution to the pleasure and to the attempted service of my life."

The management of the business would have been demanding and included master minding the development of a considerable number of Liverpool houses covering a vast area in south Liverpool and other places. Relationships with a large number of Welsh builders would have been crucial and not always easy. Trevor Roberts suffered from heart weakness and this grew seriously so that eventually his life was that of an invalid but he was held in very high regard.

There was a notable General Election in July 1892 at which the Liberals gained 80 seats. John Roberts retired from Parliament that year. Herbert Lewis, having done remarkable work as Chairman of the new Flintshire County Council and being a leading member of the "young Wales" group was elected to his Flint Boroughs seat.

Herbert Roberts took a somewhat different route but was elected to the West Denbigh seat, which he held unopposed until his retirement from the Commons in 1919. He had been busy since his father had directed his wishes in 1885. He helped his father in strenuous re-election campaigns in 1885 and 1886 learning much from that experience. He also had to learn the family business in Liverpool. In 1889 he had stood as Liberal candidate for Abergele in the first County Council Election under the new Local Government Act and was elected but found that business and other engagements limited his County Council work. However Thomas Gee, a leading Calvinistic Methodist minister, journalist and politician and proprietor of the most influential of the many journals that flourished in non-conformist Wales, the "Baner" had spotted him. Gee clearly appreciated his wealth and status as well as his faith, and suggested that he put his name forward to stand for West Denbighshire. The previous Liberal MP had become unacceptable because of his Unionist sympathies. Two other candidates Mr AC Humphreys Owen (later MP for Montgomeryshire) and Mr R Foulkes Griffiths had also been submitted and all three had to make speeches before a vote was taken. He was selected by an overwhelming majority and recorded "Thus very happily but quite unexpectedly for me, my Parliamentary Career began".

During the same period his interest in the temperance movement led him into a deep friendship and political alliance with the Caine family. His father's great achievement in securing the passing of the Sunday Closing Law was, no doubt, a powerful influence. This took a new lease of life during his world tour.

Sir Herbert Lewis, MP   Herbert Roberts, MP

Although Herbert Lewis and Herbert Roberts had been companions on the bulk of their world tour they followed rather different journeys into Parliament. In 1886 on return from the word tour Herbert Lewis formed a close working relationship with Tom Ellis, Lloyd George and Owen M. Edwards. They were all very keen and as a group they established themselves as leaders of "Young Wales". They wanted no less than "a free religion for a free people in a free land". They were to be a significant force at the centre of events for years to come. Herbert Lewis established his reputation as a person of special ability in the Chairmanship of the newly established Flintshire County Council and this led to his selection for the Flint Boroughs seat.

Welsh non-conformist religion and Welsh Liberal politics were closely entwined; although the Liberal politics also embraced economic interests for free trade. This is amply demonstrated in the life of John Roberts and he passed both deep religious faith and a belief in applying Liberal principles in the political life of the nation on to Herbert. The history of the non-conformist resurgence went back, as Herbert recalled, to events of the 1730s. Preaching by Howel Harris and Daniel Rowland created fervor in areas where Griffith Jones had established temporary schools teaching Welsh. This attracted large congregations and had a theatrical quality. The growth in the number of chapels was rapid. It was estimated that in 1851 one chapel was completed every eight days. The rise in numbers was fortified by a distinctively Welsh theology. Around 1800 the work of theologians such as Thomas Charles of Bala and

Thomas Jones of Denbigh created a high volume of popular Welsh religious publications and were an important resource for the many Sunday Schools. By that time non-conformity had become a popular mass movement bringing with it a powerful political agenda covering education, temperance, disestablishment of the Church, reform of land legislation and self-government.

As the nineteenth Century moved on several events built up the pressure. The ignorant insensitivity of the English in two particular examples provoked widespread anger but led to positive responses in the longer term. In 1847 three Education Commissioners created deep revulsion in their notorious "Blue Books" by writing in terms that were a serious condemnation of Welsh literature, language and religion. In 1859 evictions of tenants on the Rhiwlas Estate in the Merioneth Constituency for voting for their Liberal produced, according to Tom Ellis MP, "a thrill of horror throughout the countryside". The 1860s were a period, according to the eminent Welsh historian Kenneth Morgan "a period of increasingly intense ferment". The numbers of non- conformist communicants steadily grew. All this provided fertile ground for the Liberals in Wales. By succeeding in his campaign for Sunday Closing in 1881 John Roberts had shown that separate laws for Wales could be made. In 1890, Tom Ellis (a close friend of both Herbert Roberts and Herbert Lewis, who had been elected in the 1886 General Election, made a speech in Bala calling for a legislative assembly for Wales and became the Home leader of the Cymru Fydd movement seeking to gain Home Rule for Wales.

The 1892 General Election at which both Herbert Roberts and Herbert Lewis were first elected and William Sproston Caine was Member for Barrow East, was a great triumph for the Liberal Party. With the support of the Irish Nationalists Gladstone was able to form his fourth and last government. " "Young Wales" including Tom Ellis, David Lloyd George and Herbert Lewis were in there. Expectations for real social reform in Wales were very high but the going was to be complicated and tough. The 1892 -96 Parliament was to be a watershed for Welsh nationalism. In reality the demand for separatism was shallow and Cymru Fydd disintegrated. Kenneth Morgan comments on the change in Welsh radicalism "It gradually came to shed its nationalist colouring, leaving only a bitter memory to poison the future course of the Welsh national movement. The "Young Wales" MPs were all to gain high office, Lloyd George becoming Prime Minister in December 1916 and Herbert Lewis becoming a Lord of the Treasury in 1905 and Parliamentary Secretary to the Board of Education 1915-22. Tom Ellis made a very difficult decision to accept the post of Second Government Whip which meant that he was in an influential position but unable to remain within Cymru Fydd. Herbert Roberts did not position himself at the cutting edge of radical Welsh politics preferring to take on more neutral, conciliatory roles being Secretary or Chairman of various bodies including the inclusive group of Welsh MPs referred to as "The Welsh Parliamentary Party" which was not a political party.

In his memoir Herbert Roberts looked back on the collapse of the self-rule issue with a degree of detachment. He confronted the reality of long periods of government with a Conservative majority creating an injustice that could only be remedied by separate legislative machinery for Wales and mentioned the 1917 attempt by E T John MP to launch a Bill for Welsh Home Rule in 1914. This however, had little support and was overtaken by the war, he clearly saw "the special claims of Wales to a further measure of selfgovernment in education and licensing".

Herbert records that the four principal objectives of the Liberal Party in Wales during his time in the House as: -
   (i)   The Disestablishment of the Church
   (ii)   Separate Land Legislation
   (iii)   Self –Government
   (iv)   Education

He "reserved for separate treatment" two questions, which have occupied a prominent place in my Parliamentary life; namely Temperance and India.

On Disestablishment Herbert recalled "One of the earliest recollections of my boyhood was the place given to this question by Wales". It was achieved eventually in The Welsh Church Act 1914 (one of the rare Acts passed under the provisions of the Parliament Act 1911 because of opposition within the House of Lords) but the struggle had been long, hard and traumatic.

The greatest trauma was in the Welsh Parliamentary revolt of 1894 where Herbert Lewis himself with Lloyd George and two others decided to vote against the Government. Herbert described this as the first serious anxiety of his Parliamentary life. He wrote that "I had entered Parliament as the representative of a constituency whose deepest interest was the Disestablishment Bill, and many of my greatest friends and strongest political supporters were in full accord with the Revolt movement." As Tom Ellis was a Whip he had to support the Government and Herbert felt that "on personal and other grounds" he had to give great weight to his judgment. The position of Herbert Lewis was one of extreme frustration – he stated "My recent talks with Ministers and Members have convinced me that we have nothing to gain by subservience to the Liberal Party, and that we shall never get the English to do us justice until we show our independence from them." This episode embittered relations between the Welsh Members. A Disestablishment Bill was introduced and created great friction in a highly complicated situation. Welsh members were active in what turned out to be a deathblow to the Government and it fell on June 1895 and the ensuing General election was disastrous for the Liberals. The Conservatives won and the Liberals were out of power until December 1905 when Balfour resigned.

The Disestablishment issue ran on. Even after the Act had been passed there were grave difficulties about its commencement date. Herbert Roberts had the satisfaction when on 15 March 1916, as Chairman of the Welsh Parliamentary Party, he explained to the House of Commons the Party's attitude to a Postponement Bill. That Bill was then dropped.

On Welsh Land Reform the 1892 Government felt compelled to take some action but there was intense argument as to the nature of that action. The outcome, following a struggle and very strong interventions by Tom Ellis, Herbert Lewis and Lloyd George was that a Royal Commission was appointed. This carried out a major exercise. The Landlords had better representation and two completely contrasting pictures emerged. The Commission did not report until after the Government had fallen. Herbert recorded that the majority report recommendations were embodied in a Welsh Land Bill which was submitted to the Commons on many occasions and that "Having regard to the political complexion of the party in power after 1885 the passing of such legislation was, of course, out of the question and as time went on other forces came into play which materially modified the situation in regard to land in Wales." He states that the Liberals took full advantage of the Local Government Act of 1888 recording that "this development of local self-government tended to create a spirit of greater independence amongst the agricultural population in Wales, and to that extent affected the position with regard to land reform." He also commented that many tenant farmers became owners by purchasing their property.

A belief in the value of education has been almost a defining characteristic of all members of the Roberts family, continuing with commitment to this day. Herbert's memoirs have an element of ecstasy and agony on this topic. He was clearly very proud of the progress and prominence of education in Wales but he "deeply deplored that upon a question of such vital importance the best interests of the nation there should have been for so many years these acute political and sectarian difference of opinion." The detail of this is unrewarding history but it is worthwhile appreciating the overall progress as he saw it. In 1888 there were merely 30 secondary schools with 1,800 scholars whilst in 1937 there were over 160 Schools with some 40,000 scholars. In University Education in 1892 the University College at Aberystwyth had 200 students whilst in 1937 there were four University Colleges with over 3,000 students and the University of Wales was incorporated by Royal Charter in 1893.

The presence of Sir Herbert Lewis as Parliamentary Secretary to the Board of Education from 1915-22 was, undoubtedly, a very positive factor for Welsh education both in detail and in making progress despite the political and sectarian problems. He worked with the President of the Board of Education H A L Fisher on the Education Act of 1918 and the Libraries Act of 1919.In addition he was a major force behind the establishment of the Welsh National Library and the Welsh National Museum.

The Liverpool Welsh Temperance Society had been formed in Pall Mall in 1832 in response to the very high and increasing levels of drunkenness in the city. Herbert Robert's family had long been involved in the quest to eliminate this loss of human potential. It is not easy to convey an understanding of the great importance of the Temperance movement to the key figures in the Welsh Liberal party and to the non-conformists especially as it started to wane over 80 years ago. It became a worrying force to the power of the brewery interests it was opposing. For Herbert Roberts it was a pervasive influence on his life. His path to an understanding of political activity was his father's leading role in the passing of the Welsh Sunday Closing Act of 1881 when he was 18. His memoirs record that his world tour drew him in the Temperance direction with some interesting observations. He observed the Temperance question "in the life and development of the countries through which I passed, but it also opened my eyes to the importance of developing a strong citizenship at home". His rather special friendship with Sproston Caine and marriage to his daughter Hannah, who was an ardent advocate of Temperance, was a further clinching factor.

The biography of Caine by John Newton gives us the best clues as to what the Temperance movement was actually about. It was all embracing. Imagine a passionate cause with the present emphasis on "well-being" and the fervour of the many charities working with drug addicts. Caine was persuaded of the importance of Temperance when he accidentally came across, whilst in

Shrewsbury of a book "Haste to the Rescue" in which a clergy-man's wife as "an appeal to the educated classes, in true Victorian style, to take up the total abstinence movement as the only certain way of saving the masses from their own vices." Caine was influenced by many practical examples from his own work and especially by the lax administration of the Licensing Laws in Liverpool with consequent drunkenness, debauchery and crime. He agitated and a medical report into the terrible death rate was commissioned. This confirmed the extent of the problem (38% per 1,000 population, compared with Bristol's 22% and London's 24%) and traced it to the "great intemperance" of the people. This caused a sensation and led to proper administration of the Licensing laws. Caine became the equivalent of a celebrity in the growing world of the Temperance movement coming to preside over a range of bodies. The strength of the liquor lobby in Parliament was so great in 1865 that when William Lawson, Liberal MP introduced a Permissive Bill relating to the permissive prohibition of liquor traffic in 1865 only one member rose to support him. Wisely Herbert Roberts saw it as important that he should specialize in one or two subjects in order to be effective and he clearly had no regrets about his choice of Temperance and India. His memoirs are full of attendances and speeches at a mass of Temperance Meetings, and his Parliamentary career shows many occasions when vigilance on the Licensing front was important. He was appointed to the Royal Commission on Licensing in 1896 which produced many recommendations which reached the Statute book. He was also heavily involved in the 1906 Licensing Bill issuing a manifesto on Welsh Temperance Policy. His interest in the Temperance cause converged with his other special interest in India.

India made a deep impression on Herbert during his world tour. Two aspects stand out. First that the visit, lasting nearly a month, to the significant Welsh Calvinist Missionary work in the Khasi Hill of Aswan was, probably, the highlight of his journey around the world and secondly that he found the British rule in India deeply questionable.

Throughout his career Herbert pursued his Indian concerns with determination. There is no doubt that he treasured his contacts with Indians, many of them very senior figures. Just after visiting Benares, he wrote "of the difficulty for an English politician to form a right estimate of the Indian question, even if he was disposed to do so at all". He repeated this in his memoir. It is easy to understand his thought on this and its force. As a young graduate with his family background he would have been highly conscious of the almost complete disregard and lack of understanding Westminster had for Welsh interests. The impact of experiencing a vast country with a population then of over 250 million must have stretched his mind. The same thoughts engaged the practical mind of Sproston Caine. Caine framed his robust critique on three themes. First, with his belief in temperance, he was fiercely critical of the encouragement, for fiscal purposes, of the liquor and opium trade and he attacked this with vigour. Secondly, whilst recognizing many benefits of British rule, he made a detailed and persuasive substantial critique of policies toward Indian poverty. Thirdly he was a strong advocate of Indian self- government.

The Anglo-Indian Temperance Society formed by Caine and Samuel Smith MP in 1888 on Caine's return from his world tour brought Herbert and Caine together. Caine worked with great energy to ventilate in Parliament the grievances that a large number of Hindus had put to him in a meeting in Bombay earlier that year. He returned to India on behalf of the Society and addressed nearly 100 meetings, some of enormous proportions. When Caine lost his seat in Bradford in 1895 Herbert resolved to represent his views in the House for his five years absence "as well as he was able". When Caine died in 1903 Herbert was invited to succeed him as Treasurer and Hon Secretary of the Society and became President in April 1910. On wider questions relating to Indian rule and finances Herbert spoke on the Indian Budget every year from 1896 and intervened on many Indian questions.

Herbert Lewis was also an ardent supporter of the Indian cause and shared the Indian connections and friendship with Sproston Caine and Herbert Roberts. Among the influential Indians with whom the extended family formed friendships was Gopal Krsihna Gokhale. He was one of the social and political leaders of the Independence movement being a senior leader of the Indian National Congress and was a mentor to both Ghandi and Jinnah. He founded the Servants of India Society, which organized many campaigns to promote education, sanitation, and health care and fight the social evils of untouchability and discrimination, alcoholism, poverty, oppression of women and domestic abuse. Another family friend was Romesh Chunder Dutt a highly respected senior Indian civil servant, economic historian, writer and politician. The friendship of the family with its radical determination and presence in the British Parliament must have been a considerable comfort to these eminent Indians.

The Welsh missionary work in Khasi was on a par with the Welsh emigration to Patagonia. Less than a decade after the British conquered the Khasi Hills in Assam dozens of Welsh missionaries, almost magnetized by the remoteness of the area, travelled the perilous journey there and by 1901 there were also 20,000 converts out of a Khasi population of 100,000. In his journal Herbert Roberts wrote that few Welshmen had not heard of Khasis and his five Chapters about the area show real warmth for the area, its people, the Welsh singing he heard ("as hearty as I ever heard at home"), the scenic beauty and his admiration for the work of the missionaries. The Liverpool element in the work arose because the London Missionary Society had refused the request of Thomas Jones of Montgomeryshire (1810-1849) to support his applications to work India but Liverpool Welsh Calvinistic Methodists who formed their own Foreign Mission supported him. Their meeting on 14 November was crowned with a hymn-like poem "With a tuneful joyous note let the Hills of Khasia resound". David Roberts was amongst the supporters. It would be odd if he had not passed a vivid memory of this occasion on to his grandson Herbert.

The linguistic skills stamina and determination of Thomas Jones made a lasting impact upon Khasi society. In 1884 the trio of travellers witnessed the impact, Herbert Roberts writing that "The Khasi Christians, like their dwellings are always neat and clean in outward appearance, with bright and happy countenances, but the heathen are quite the reverse of this, and so are their houses." He found difficulty in "tearing himself away from the Mission House in Shillong" but clearly enjoyed the scenery of the onward journey "extremely grand, great mountain chains, dark gloomy chasms, a rich sunset".

Going forward in time the public role of Herbert Roberts changed when he was elevated to the peerage in 1919. By that date the Liberal Party was a weakened force but Herbert carried on with a round of activity as a person of influence in North Wales. In his memoir he states adamantly "Let me emphasise the fact that the inspiration of all my Parliamentary endeavours has come from the principles and ideals of the Liberal Party". He gives us an understanding of an important aspect of what he means by "Liberal principles" in a very interesting comment on "our lack of understanding of national psychology in the solution of national and international problems". He applies this directly to Ireland and India.

Looking back at the process of decline there were undoubtedly deep tensions between what the Welsh Liberals wanted for Wales and what the English Liberals were prepared to concede. In 1892 Gladstone himself played a fickle hand. On the one hand, on a picturesque occasion under Snowdon he spoke with warmth about Welsh nationhood but within a few months proved most intransigent on pressing Welsh issues. The high hopes, which the 1892 Liberal Government raised in Wales, came to relatively little and the great tension between Welsh and other Liberals materially led to the downfall of the government in 1895. Then followed ten years of Conservative domination with very little sympathy for Welsh interests. The 1906 Liberal government again raised Welsh hopes and the Liberals remained strong in Wales, defying Labour inroads from the industrial southern valleys until 1914. The huge energy of Lloyd George was, during that period, focused on what the Welsh Liberals had sought in terms of justice and social welfare. His reforming "Peoples Budget" of 1908 took this as far as he thought he could at the time. Herbert Lewis was a close and loyal mentor to Lloyd George and both he and Herbert Roberts supported him to the end of his career. The friendship between the two Herberts continued all their lives but Herbert Lewis operated in a different way and was one of those rare politicians who manage to be effective, get things done with genuine integrity and be highly effective in practical terms. Disregarding Lloyd George, who he supported and mentored, he is arguably the leading Welsh politician of the period.

In 1937 at the end of his memoir Herbert Roberts was still able to take a positive note – "Liberalism is not dead and I am convinced more than ever that it is only through the penetration of Liberal principles into the political life of the nation that we will safely guide the ship of state through the perilous seas of the near future." Herbert Roberts took a religious view of life and this appears to have inhibited what he could write about with comfort. There is no mention of his commercial work or how the family money was made. For a memoir about a period during which war was, for most people the dominant, often devastating issue the absence of reference to war save for the notable speech of Sir Edward Grey prior to the outbreak of the second world war seems strange. The memoir was written in 1937 and most politicians at that time were acutely conscious of the risk of war again.

Lord Clwyd

The Welsh politicians spent the Parliamentary season on London. This brought them together in a way that the Welsh geography inhibited. They had a convivial life together. Much deep discussion and debate was match by a convivial social life.

Herbert Roberts was certainly involved in commercial life. In addition to his involvement in the family land development enterprise he was a Director of two major concerns. In the building trade he was a Director of the major builders and civil engineers Costains. During his period of Directorship they built Dolphin Square, described by Pevsner as "largest self-contained block of flats in Europe", as well as many large housing estates and civil engineering works abroad. Dolphin Square pace great financial strain on the company and It is quite possible that Herbert was a quiet but important influence in their difficult relations with their bankers. He was also a Director of the United Kingdom Temperance and Provident Institution where he found comfort in the virtues of temperance from a financial point of view.

The memoir gives the impression of life of routine somewhat detached from the realities of the world. There is a feel of a gentle ongoing annual pattern to his life and the routine at Bryngwenallt cut off from troubling questions. He moved from Tanyrallt to Bryngwenallt, apparently with a degree of reluctance only in 1900. Remarkably one of the preparations was the installation of electricity there, some twenty years ahead of the time and managed by a nephew of Tom Ellis MP. He recorded enigmatically that his purchase of the Clausen painting "The Harrow" had some relation to our decision to move". The routine at Bryngwenallt must have been full of some wonderful occasions. Herbert was very popular in the area. Politicians and preachers were welcome visitors. The organ in the magnificent great hall must have enabled some fine and powerful music – on one occasion there was a performance for which Herbert's brother Osborne wrote the music and brother-in-law William Caine the words. Herbert's status as a local figure, a Welsh speaking non-conformist Lord, giving support and help to many local organisations would have been of real value to the social cohesion of a wide area.

Of John's twelve children only two had issue. Herbert himself had three sons and Meinwen, his fourth daughter, had two sons and two daughters. These lines are full of a diversity of remarkable and interesting people and it can be said with confidence that a great spirit lives on.

Descendants of David Roberts

GŴYL DAVID ROBERTS – COFIO CEWRI OES VICTORIA gan
Arthur Thomas

Cynhaliwyd yr ŵyl i ddathlu bywyd a gwaith David Roberts a'i ddisgynyddion ar y pen wythnos Mehefin 11-12 gyda darlithiau yn y bore yng Nghapel Bethel a'r Ganolfan Gymraeg, cyngerdd yn yr hwyr yng nghapel Elm Hall Drive a gwasanaeth o ddiolchgarwch bore Sul ym Methel. Trefnwyd yr ŵyl gan Gymdeithas Etifeddiaeth Cymry Glannau Mersi dan arweiniad Dr D. Ben Rees, ac mewn cydweithrediad gyda Dr Lawrence Holden, Penbedw, yn cynrychioli disgynyddion David Roberts.

Paratowyd arddangosfa ddiddorol ganddo gan gynnwys siart o achau y teulu ers dyddiau David Roberts, lluniau o ddau gartref y teulu gerllaw Abergele sef Tanrallt a Bryngwenallt , a nifer o eitemau diddorol eraill yn enwedig y ddogfen gyfreithiol drawiadol yn dyrchafu John Herbert Roberts yn Farwn Clwyd yn 1919.

Rhoddwyd y ddarlith gyntaf yn yr Iaith Gymraeg ar David Roberts (1806 - 1886) a'i fab John Roberts, A.S. (1835 - 1894) gan Dr D Ben Rees. Cefais y fraint o gyflwyno'r darlithydd oedd wedi gweithio'n galed ar yr ymchwil gan mae ychydig iawn oedd yn wybyddus am y marsiandwr coed a'i fab y gwleidydd Rhydfrydol . Trefnwyd gwasanaeth cyfieithu ar y pryd gan y Gymdeithas ac fe werthfawrogwyd y cyfleuster yma yn fawr gan nifer dda o'r teulu oedd wedi dod i'r Ŵyl o bob rhan o'r wlad.

Yn dilyn ei fagwraeth yn Llanrwst daeth David Roberts i Lerpwl yn ddyn ifanc iawn yn 1822 ac ymhen ychydig flynyddoedd roedd wedi sefydlu cwmni yn mewnforio coed gan arbennigo mewn coed mahogani.

Aeth y fusnes o nerth i nerth. Or cychwyn bu yn aelod o gapel Bedford Street ac yn fuan etholwyd ef i'r Sedd Fawr a bu yn flaenor weddill ei oes, hyd ei farwolaeth yn 1886. Ei ddymuniad mawr oedd adeiladu capel, teilwng o safle y Cymry yn y ddinas. Sicrhaodd ei benderfyniad, gan mai hwy oedd berchen y tir a brynodd oddiwrth Iarll Sefton, a'i gefnogaeth ariannol, adeiladu capel urddasol Princes Road. Agorwyd y capel yn 1868.

Ymunodd ei fab John Roberts yn y busnes a'i ddatblygu ymhellach gan gydweithio gyda'r pensaer dylanwadol Richard Owen . Yn 1878 etholwyd ef yn Aelod Seneddol Rhyddfrydol dros Bwrdeisdrefi Sir Fflint ac fe wnaeth gyfraniad sylweddol i sicrhau y mesur cau y tafarnau ar y Sul yng Nghymru erbyn 1881.

Yn dilyn egwyl cafwyd darlith ddiddorol arall gan Dr Lawrence Holden ar ddau o ddisgynyddion David Roberts sef, David Trevor Roberts a John Herbert Roberts, A.S., yn ddiweddarach y Barwn Clwyd, a hefyd dau wleidydd arall sef teulu Caine a Syr Herbert Lewis .Canolbwyntiodd David Trevor Roberts ar ddatblygu y cwmni ac yn 1906 etholwyd John Herbert Roberts yn Aelod Seneddol dros Sir Fflint, a'i ddyrchafu yn Farwn Clwyd yn 1919.

Bwriedir cyhoeddi y ddwy ddarlith hynod bwysig yma mewn llyfr yn y dyfodol agos, a byddwn yn hysbysebu yn ol ein harfer yn yr Angor.

Yn yr hwyr bu cyngerdd cofiadwy yng nghapel Elm Hall Drive gyda Côr y Porthmyn o ardal y Rhewl, ger Rhuthun. Dan arweiniad Erfyl Owen, cyflwynwyd y rhaglen apelgar gan Gwynfor Jones. Cafwyd unawdau gan John Jones, Geraint Evans, John Thomas, Wyn Jones, Brian Hughes a Eirlys Jones. Yn ystod yr egwyl rhoddwyd datganiad gan Mrs Rhiannon Liddell ar y piano o ddarn a gyfansoddwyd gan Mervyn Roberts, trydydd mab Arglwydd Clwyd. Yn dilyn gair o werthfawrogiad gan Mrs Alice Brown, Glasgow, ar ran y teulu, cafwyd datganiad gwefreiddiol gan Barnaby Brown ar y '*triplepipes*'. Roedd yn offeryn digon cyffredin yn y byd Celtaidd yn y canol oesoedd, ac mae'r defnydd ohonno yn parhau yn Sardinia. Llywyddwyd gan y Dr D.Ben Rees yn ei afiaith ei hun ac yn hyfryd o ddi-rybudd mynegodd Mr Brian Thomas, Mossley Hill, aelod o Bwyllgor Gwaith y Gymdeithas, werthfawrogiad didwyll o weledigaeth ein Llywydd Dr Ben ar hyd y blynyddoedd ac yn arbennig gyda Gwyl David Roberts ac eiliwyd hyn gan gyfeirio at y criw bach sydd yn ysgwyddo y cyfrifoldeb gan Ted Clement–Evans, Aigburth. O blith chwiorydd y Pwyllgor Gwaith sef Dr Pat Williams, Mrs Nan Hughes Parry a Mrs Beryl Williams porthwyd y porthmyn yn unol a thraddodiad Cymry Lerpwl gyda lluniaeth blasus. Noson gofiadwy iawn.

Ar fore Sul bu gwasanaeth o ddiolchgarwch ym Methel dan arweiniad y gweinidog, Dr Ben Rees, gyda Mrs Rhiannon Liddell wrth yr organ. Cymerwyd rhan gan aelodau o bwyllgor Cymdeithas Etifeddieth Cymry Glannau Mersi,mewn gwasanaeth a baratowyd yn ofalus ac a argraffwyd ar gyfer y gynulleidfa deilwng a ddaeth ynghyd. Roedd hynny yn wir ym mhob cyfarfod a gafwyd .

Cymdeithas Etifeddiaeth Cymry Glannau Mersi
(Merseyside Welsh Heritage Society)   ac Eglwysi
Presbyteraidd Cymraeg Glannau Mersi.
Gŵyl teulu David Roberts (1806-1886),
Hope Street, Lerpwl ac Abergele.

Oedfa i ddiolch am farsiandwyr
ym myd coed ac adeiladu.

Bore Sul, 12 Mehefin 2016 am 10.30 o'r gloch yn
Eglwys Bresbyteraidd Cymru, Bethel,
Heathfield Road/Auckland Road, Lerpwl.

Llywydd: Parchedig Athro D. Ben Rees.

Organydd: Mrs Rhiannon Liddell.

Trefn yr Oedfa / Order of Service

Intrada
Croeso i'r oedfa gan y Llywydd.

Ymateb y Gynulleidfa i'r alwad i addoli (y Gynulleidfa i ganu ac i adrodd
yr ymateb).

Canu ar y dôn *Nicea*.
Sanctaidd, sanctaidd, Dduw hollalluog,
Gyda gwawr y bore, dyrchafwn fawl i ti,
Sanctaidd, sanctaidd, sanctaidd, cadarn a thrugarog, Trindod fendigaid
yw ein Harglwydd ni.

Adrodd:
I ti, Arglwydd sanctaidd, y cyflwynwn ein moliant a'n gweddiau yn yr
addoliad hwn yn awr.
Molwn di ar dy holl ymwneud grasol â ni; am i ti ein
creu ar dy lun a'th ddelw dy hun; am i ti ein cynnal a'n

cadw yn dy gariad; am i ti ein gwaredu, O Arglwydd ein
Duw, yn dy fab Iesu Grist; am i ti drigo gyda ni yn
wastad yng ngrym dy Ysbryd Glân.

Canu : ar y dôn *Ysbryd y Tragwyddol Dduw*.

Ysbryd y tragwyddol Dduw, disgyn arnom ni;
ysbryd y tragwyddol Dduw, disgyn arnom ni;
plyg ni, trin ni, cod ni: ysbryd y tragwyddol
Dduw, disgyn arnom ni.

Darlleniad o'r Hen Destament: Llyfr Job, pennod 38, adnodau 3
– 35. (Darlleniad gan Mrs Nan Hughes Parry).

Emyn 1 : Rhif 319 yn Caneuon Ffydd. (i'w
ddarllen gan Rachel Gooding).

> Wele'n sefyll rhwng y myrtwydd
> wrthrych teilwng o'm holl fryd,
> er mai o ran yr wy'n adnabod
> ei fod uwchllaw gwrthrychau'r byd:
> henffych fore
> y caf ei weled fel y mae.

> Rhosyn Saron yw ei enw,
> gwyn a gwridog, teg o bryd;
> ar ddeng mil y mae'n rhagori
> o wrthrychau penna'r byd:
> ffrind pechadur,
> dyma ei beilot ar y môr.

> Beth sydd imi mwy a wnelwyf
> ag eilunod gwael y llawr?
> Tystio 'rwyf nad yw eu cwmni
> i'w gystadlu â'm Iesu mawr:
> O am aros
> yn ei gariad ddyddiau f'oes.

Ann Griffiths.

Myfyrdod: Adeiladu Capel Mynydd Seion, Abergele a Chapel Princes Road, Lerpwl. (i'w ddarllen gan Mrs Elin Bryn Boyd).

Prif ysgogydd adeiladu'r capel newydd Mynydd Seion, Abergele, oedd David Roberts. Digwyddodd hyn yn 1869. Ond cofier mae dim ond blwyddyn oedd wedi mynd heibio ers agor Eglwys hardd Princes Road yn Lerpwl a'r un person oedd yn ysgogi yr adeiladu hwnnw. Hwn oedd adeilad harddaf Lerpwl. Cynlluniwyd Princes Road ar ffurf croes, yn gan troedfedd o hyd, ac yn bedwar ugain troedfedd o led ar draws breichiau'r groes, y *transepts*. Ar y llawr yr oedd eisteddleoedd i naw cant o wrandawyr, a daliai'r tair oriel, un yn y pen draw, a dwy bob ochr i'r pulpud, oddeutu 350. Uwchben y prif fynedfa, roedd tŵr hardd a chymesur yn ymgodi i uchder o yn agos i ddau can troedfedd. Nid rhyfedd i'r adeilad godidog hwn gael ei alw yn syth yn *Gathedral* – Eglwys Gadeiriol y Methodistiaid Calfinaidd Cymraeg ar lannau Mersi.

A phan edrychwn ar restr y cyfranwyr i adeiladu'r Capel hwn gwelwn mae David Roberts a'i fab John Roberts, y ddau flaenor, oedd caredigion yr achos. Y pennaf oedd David Roberts, a gyfrannodd fil o bunnoedd, a chyfrannodd ei fab, John Roberts y swm o £500. Dwy flynedd yn ddiweddarach cafwyd yr un stori o haelioni anghyffredin. Dyhead y ddau oedd cael adeiladau hardd i addoli y Creawdwr, yr Hollalluog Dduw.

Ond ar yr un adeg penderfynodd y ddau, y tad a'r mab, adeiladu Capel hardd yn Abergele lle yr oeddent wedi cartrefu gyda'i ail gartref. Gwahoddwyd Richard Owen, Lerpwl, fel pensaer y capel newydd. Cynllun Gothig sydd i'r capel, ac fe'i adeiladwyd â narthecs, aleau croes a thalcen crwn, a galeri yn y cefn. Roedd y gost bron yn £4,000 tra roedd y gost yn Princes Road bron yn £20,000, pum gwaith mwy nag adeiladu Mynydd Seion. Ond gwnaed llawer o'r gwaith yn wirfoddol yn Abergele gan wyth ar hugain o ffermwyr lleol yn cludo defnyddiau ar gyfer yr adeiladu o'r gloddfa ac o'r rheilffordd yn Mhensarn. (A sôn am Pensarn, cofier i David a John Roberts adeiladu yn 1877 Gapel Saesneg ym Mhensarn, a thalu amdano, a'i gyflwyno yn rhodd i'r enwad).

Richard Owen a'r Robertsiaid oedd yn gyfrifol am yr ysgoldy fechan a adeiladwyd yn 1887 mewn dull newydd cyffrous. Bu cysylltiad agos rhwng David Roberts a chapel Bedford Street a Princes Road am 50 mlynedd, ac am 30 mlynedd gyda Mynydd Seion. Gweinidogion a fu yn weinidogion ar David Roberts a'i fab yn Lerpwl oedd Parch John Hughes, Dr David Saunders, Dr Owen Thomas, ac yn Abergele, William Roberts (1869-1883) a Francis Jones (1889-1913).

Bu ŵyr David Roberts, John Herbert Roberts, Barwn cyntaf Clwyd, yn aelod Seneddol Gorllewin Clwyd o 1892-1918. Bu hefyd yn flaenor ym Mynydd Seion am 68 o flynyddoedd, o 1887 i 1955. Roedd John Roberts yn gefnogwr brwd dros achosion Saesneg y Methodistiaid Calfinaidd ond un o'i brif wrthwynebwyr oedd Robert Ambrose Jones (Emrys ap Iwan) a gychwynodd bregethu ym Mynydd Seion ac a fu'n dysgu plant yr eglwys yn yr Ysgol Sul o 1876 hyd 1883.

Reflections: Building Mynydd Seion Chapel, Abergele, and Princes Road Chapel, Liverpool.

David Roberts was the main influence behind the building of the new chapel of Mynydd Seion, Abergele, in 1869. It is worth noting that only a few years had elapsed since the opening of the handsome chapel of Princes Road in Liverpool, where David Roberts had also led the initiative. This was one of Liverpool's most striking buildings. It was designed in the form of a cross, a hundred feet long and eighty feet wide across the arms of the cross, the transepts. It could accommodate 900 worshippers with a further 350 in the three galleries at the rear and to the sides. Over the main entrance there was an elegant spire rising to some 200 feet. Little wonder that this new building soon became known as the 'Cathedral' of the Welsh Methodist cause in Liverpool.

When we look at the list of contributors to finance the building of the chapel David Roberts and his son John Roberts, two elders, led the benefactions. David Roberts donated a thousand pounds and his son John five hundred pounds. Some two years later they displayed the same kind of generosity in order to ensure the building of a worthy chapel for God's worship.

At around the same time the two, father and son, decided to build an impressive chapel in Abergele, where they had established a second home at Bryngwenallt. Richard Owen, Liverpool, was engaged as architect. The new chapel had a Gothic design, built with a narthex, transepts and an apse with a gallery to the rear. It cost nearly £4,000, while the cost of Princes Road was some £20,000, five times the figure for Mynydd Seion. Much of the work in Mynydd Seion was volunteered by 28 local farmers who transported materials from nearby quarries and the railway station at Pensarn. (And speaking of Pensarn, David and John Roberts built a chapel for the English cause there in 1877 and presented it to the connexion). Richard Owen and the Roberts' were also responsible for building the small schoolroom in 1887 in a new modern style.

David Roberts had a fifty-year connection with the chapels of Bedford street and Princes Road, and for some thirty years with Mynydd Seion. In Liverpool David Roberts and his son worshipped under several famous Liverpool ministers--the Rev. John Hughes, Dr. David Saunders, Dr. Owen Thomas and in Abergele, William Roberts (1869-1883) and Francis Jones (1889-1913). David Roberts' grandson, John Herbert Roberts, 1st Baron Clwyd represented West Clwyd in the House of Commons from 1892-1918. He was also an elder at Mynydd Seion for 68 years, from 1887 to 1955. John Roberts was an ardent supporter of the 'English causes' of the Calvinistic Methodists, while one of its main opponents was Robert Ambrose Jones (Emrys ap Iwan), who started his preaching career at Mynydd Seion, and who taught in the Sunday School from 1876 to 1883.

EMYN 2 : Rhif 517 yn Caneuon Ffydd. (i'w ddarllen gan Dr Arthur Thomas).

 Dros bechadur buost farw,
dros bechadur, ar y pren,
y dioddefaist hoelion llymion
nes it orfod crymu pen;
dwed i mi, ai fi oedd hwnnw
gofiodd cariad rhad mor fawr-
marw dros un bron â suddo
yn Gehenna boeth i lawr?

Dwed i mi, a wyt yn maddau
cwympo ganwaith i'r un bai?
Dwed a ddeui byth i galon
na all gynnig 'difarhau?
 Beth yw pwysau'r beiau mwyaf   a
faddeui? O ba ri'?
 Pa un drymaf yw fy mhechod
ai griddfannau Calfari?

Arglwydd, rhaid i mi gael bywyd;
mae fy meiau yn rhy fawr,
fy euogrwydd sy'n cydbwyso
â mynyddoedd mwya'r llawr;

rhad faddeuant, gwawria bellach,
gwna garcharor caeth yn rhydd,
fu'n ymdreiglo mewn tywyllwch,
nawr i weled golau'r dydd.

William Williams.

Darlleniad o'r Testament Newydd:
Yr Epistol at y Rhufeiniaid, pennod 8, adnodau 14 i 39. (i'w
ddarllen gan Mr Brian Thomas).

EMYN 3 : Rhif 340 yn Caneuon Ffydd.
(i'w ddarllen gan Ms Rachel Gooding)

O llefara, addfwyn Iesu,
mae dy eiriau fel y gwin,
oll yn dwyn i mewn dangnefedd
ag sydd o anfeidrol rin;
mae holl leisiau'r greadigaeth,
holl ddeniadau cnawd a byd,
wrth dy lais hyfrytaf, tawel
yn distewi a mynd yn fud.

Ni all holl hyfrydwch natur,
a'i melystra penna'i maes,
fyth gymharu â lleferydd
hyfryd, pur, maddeuol ras;
gad im glywed sŵn dy eiriau,
awdurdodol eiriau'r nef,
oddi mewn yn creu hyfrydwch
nad oes mo'i gyffelyb ef.

Dwed dy fod yn eiddo imi,
mewn llythrennau eglur, clir;
tor amheuaeth sych, digysur,
tywyll, dyrys, cyn bo hir;
'rwy'n hiraethu am gael clywed
un o eiriau pur y ne',

nes bod ofon du a thristwch
yn tragwyddol golli eu lle.

William Williams

**Gweddi ac yn dilyn Gweddi'r Arglwydd o dan ofal Dr Pat
Williams.**

**Llywydd y Mis : Cyhoeddiadau a'r Casgliad. Gweddi ar
yr Offrwm.**

EMYN 4 : Rhif 813 yn Caneuon Ffydd. (i'w
ddarllen gan Dr Arthur Thomas)

O dduw, a'n creaist ar dy lun
yn weithwyr fel tydi dy hun,
derbyn ein llafur ni yn awr yn
foliant byth i'th enw mawr.

Ti fu'n cysegru mainc y saer â'th
ddiwyd waith a'th weddi daer;
sancteiddia ni, a dyro fod ein gwaith
a'n gweddi er dy glod.

Gelwaist rai gynt ar lan y lli i
ado'u gwaith a'th ddilyn di; rho
wybod mai ein galw'r wyd i'th
ganlyn wrth gyweirio'r rhwyd.

Mewn craig a phwll, ynghanol sŵn
peiriannau a'u byddarol rŵn, rho
glywed dy leferydd di: "Gwnewch
hyn er coffa amdanaf fi."

Hawliaist i'r eiddot ger y llyn dy
garu'n fwy na'r "pethau hyn": tro
waith ein dwylo, Geidwad mwyn, yn
llafur cariad er dy fwyn.

Huw Roberts

Homili :Parchedig Ddr D. Ben Rees.

EMYN 5 : Rhif 315 yn Caneuon Ffydd (i'w
ddarllen gan Dr D. Ben Rees)

'Rwy'n dy garu, ti a'i gwyddost,
'rwy'n dy garu, f'Arglwydd mawr;
'rwy'n dy garu yn anwylach
na'r gwrthrychau ar y llawr:
        darllen yma
ar fy ysbryd waith dy law.

Fflam o dân o ganol nefoedd
yw, ddisgynnodd yma i'r byd,
 tân a lysg fy natur gyndyn,
tân a leinw f'eang fryd:
        hwn ni ddiffydd
tra parhao Duw mewn bod.

Ble'r enynnodd fy nymuniad?
Ble cadd fy serchiadau dân?
Ble daeth hiraeth im am bethau
fûm yn eu casáu o'r blaen?
        Iesu, Iesu,
    cwbwl ydyw gwaith dy law.

Dymuniadau pell eu hamcan
 'rwyn'n eu teimlo yno'i 'nglŷn;
dacw'r ffynnon bur tarddasant –
anfeidroldeb mawr ei hun:
        dyma 'ngobaith
bellach byth y cânt barhau.

William Williams

Homili : Tystiolaeth am David Roberts. (i'w ddarllen
gan Mrs Beryl Williams).

Pan ddarllenwn y wasg Gymraeg a Saesneg yn y cyfnod o 1850 i 1886 sonnir
gydag edmygedd o gyfraniad David Roberts i waith yr Efengyl yn ninas Lerpwl.
Yn y deyrnged iddo fe ddywedodd y Parchedig Francis Jones, Abergele:

"Do, yn marwolaeth y gŵr da hwn fe gollodd y Methodistiaid un o'r rhai mwyaf
o'u blaenoriaid; ac os cymerer ei holl rhagoriaethau i ystyriaeth, hwyrach nad
gormod dweud y mwyaf a fu ganddynt o ddechreuad y Gyfundeb."

Nid un sydd yn dweud hynny ond nifer eraill. Gwyddom fod David Roberts yn
hoff iawn o emynau Ann Griffiths a Williams, Pantycelyn, (emynau a glywn yn
yr oedfa hon) ond roedd ef hefyd yn hoff o farwnadau Pantycelyn. Dyfynwyd
pennill o farwnad un o gewri yr Annibynwyr, Williams o'r Wern, wrth gyfeirio
at David Roberts:-

"Pe bai tywallt dagrau'n tycio
 Er cael eto weld dy wedd,
 Ni chai aros, gallaf dystio
 Hanner munud yn dy fedd,
 Deuai'r holl eglwysi i wylo,
 A gollyngent yn y fan
 Ffrwd ddigonol i dy nofio,
 O waelodion bedd i'r lan!"

Homili: Testimony for David Roberts

When we read the Welsh and English press in the period from 1850 to 1886 the
contribution of David Roberts to the religious life of Liverpool is reported with
considerable admiration. In his tribute to David Roberts the Rev. Francis Jones,
Abergele, said;

"Yes, in the death of this good man the Methodist cause has lost one of its
greatest elders; and if we take all of his virtues into account it would not be out
of place to say he was the best they had seen from the start of the Connexion".

Others add similar testimony. We also know that David Roberts was fond of the
hymns of Ann Griffiths and William Williams, Pantycelyn (hymns sung in this

service), but he was also fond of the elegies written by William Williams, particularly one composed in memory of a leading Independent minister, Williams o'r Wern.

EMYN 6 : Rhif 724 yn Caneuon Ffydd. (i'w ddarllen gan Mrs Beryl Williams).

Er mai cwbwl groes i natur
yw fy llwybyr yn y byd,
ei deithio wnaf, a hynny'n dawel
yng ngwerthfawr wedd dy ŵyneb-pryd;
wrth godi'r groes ei chyfri'n goron,
mewn gorthrymderau llawen fyw,
ffordd yn union, er mor ddyrys,
i ddinas gyfaneddol yw.

Ffordd a'i henw yn "Rhyfeddol",
hen, a heb heneiddio, yw;
ffordd heb ddechrau, eto'n newydd,
ffordd yn gwneud y meirw'n fyw;
ffordd i ennill ei thrafaelwyr,
ffordd yn Briod, ffordd yn Ben,
ffordd gysegrwyd, af ar hyd-ddi
i orffwys ynddi draw i'r llen.

Ffordd na chenfydd llygad barcut
er ei bod fel hanner dydd,
ffordd ddisathar, anweledig
i bawb ond perchenogion ffydd;
ffordd i gyfiawnhau'r annuwiol,
ffordd i godi'r meirw'n fyw,
ffordd gyfreithlon i droseddwyr
i hedd a ffafor gyda Duw.

Ann Griffiths

Y Fendith gan Lywydd yr oedfa.

Diolch.

Diolchwn fel Cymdeithas am gydweithrediad Eglwys Bethel, yn weinidog a blaenoriaid, i'r organydd ac i bawb a gymerodd ran yn yr ŵyl hon sydd yn cofio cyfraniad pwysig teulu y gŵr a ddaeth o Lanrwst ac a fu yn rhan bwysig o lwyddiant y ddinas yn oes Victoria.

Arthur Thomas, Ysgrifennydd